Private Women and the Public Good

Private Women and the Public Good

Charity and State Formation in Hamilton, Ontario, 1846-93

Carmen J. Nielson

UBCPress · Vancouver · Toronto

22 21 20 19 18 17 16 15 14   5 4 3 2 1

Printed in Canada on FSC-certified ancient-forest-free paper (100% post-consumer recycled) that is processed chlorine- and acid-free.

Library and Archives Canada Cataloguing in Publication

Nielson, Carmen J., 1972-, author
Private women and the public good : charity and state formation in Hamilton, Ontario, 1846-93 / Carmen J. Nielson.

Includes bibliographical references and index.
Issued in print and electronic formats.
ISBN 978-0-7748-2691-4 (bound). – ISBN 978-0-7748-2692-1 (pbk.). – ISBN 978-0-7748-2693-8 (pdf). – ISBN 978-0-7748-2694-5 (epub)

1. Women in charitable work – Ontario – Hamilton – History – 19th century. 2. Ladies' Benevolent Society (Hamilton, Ont.) – History – 19th century. 3. Hamilton Orphan Asylum – History – 19th century. 4. Charities – Ontario – Hamilton – History – 19th century. 5. Public welfare – Ontario – Hamilton – History – 19th century. I. Title.

HV110.H34N53 2014   362.7309713'52   C2014-900720-5
C2014-900721-3

Canada

UBC Press gratefully acknowledges the financial support for our publishing program of the Government of Canada (through the Canada Book Fund), the Canada Council for the Arts, and the British Columbia Arts Council.

This book has been published with the help of a grant from the Canadian Federation for the Humanities and Social Sciences, through the Awards to Scholarly Publications Program, using funds provided by the Social Sciences and Humanities Research Council of Canada.

UBC Press
The University of British Columbia
2029 West Mall
Vancouver, BC V6T 1Z2
www.ubcpress.ca

To my parents

Contents

Acknowledgments

I WOULD LIKE TO extend my sincere thank you to those who have read and critiqued this work at various stages and whose influence and advice materially improved it: Jane Errington, Suzanne Morton, Jeffrey McNairn, Marguerite Van Die, Brian Osborne, Elsbeth Heaman, Harold Mah, Ian McKay, Margaret Little, Brian Young, Nancy Janovicek, Emily Hutchison, and the anonymous readers chosen by UBC Press. I would also like to recognize the research assistance of Erika Fyfe, Erin Brubacher, Josee Jamault, and Antoinette Nielson. Melissa Pitts, my editor at UBC Press, has been supportive and helpful throughout the publishing process. Thank you to *Women's History Review* and *Journal of Canadian Studies* for allowing material published in these journals to be reproduced here. I have been exceedingly fortunate to have had the support of many mentors, colleagues, and friends during my years at Queen's, McGill, St. Francis Xavier, Trent, and Mount Royal. Thank you all.

Private Women and the Public Good

Introduction
Gender and the Public Sphere

Private Women and the Public Good is a case study about a charity institution established by forty-six white, middle-class, Protestant women in Hamilton, Canada West, in 1846. This examination of two separate but jointly administered associations, the Ladies' Benevolent Society (LBS) and Hamilton Orphan Asylum (HOA), reveals tensions within nineteenth-century conceptualizations of private charity and the multitude of ways in which public institutions, from municipal councils to provincial legislatures, financed and governed charitable endeavours. Added to and overlapping with these tensions were gender ideologies that assigned the public world to men and sought to restrict women's access to the domestic sphere only. The book's title alludes to a paradox that is this study's principal focus: although nineteenth-century women's charitable work was nominally private because it was both voluntary and feminine, these efforts were sustained by public monies, legitimated by law, and served the so-called public good. The book's main argument is that while the complexity and extent of charitable associationalism's political significance has been underestimated, the challenge that women's charitable endeavours posed to the ideology of separate spheres has been overestimated.

The phenomenon of voluntary associationalism emerged with the development of civil society in the post-Enlightenment West. These associations represented a novel form of social interaction that was separate from family, church, or market wherein individual men and women came together as a group on their own accord. Associations were established for charitable, fraternal, educational, patriotic, and myriad other purposes.[1]

In British North America, immigrant aid or employment societies were among the first voluntary associations established during the settlement period.[2] Charitable associations tended to arise out of these often failed attempts to cope with destitute immigrants, particularly women and children who had been left to fend for themselves when their male protector succumbed to disease en route to the colonies. Since the Poor Laws had not been established in Upper Canada, those who could not provide for themselves had no rightful claim on the state for support.[3] Churches took on the responsibility to provide for destitute members of their congregations, and local boards of police or the courts sometimes meted out meagre bits of aid in crisis situations.

A combination of local demand for services, the existence of precedents elsewhere, and a cultural expectation that upstanding women of means would provide for the poor combined to bring the Ladies' Benevolent Society in Hamilton into being. Throughout the nineteenth century, these women, and those who followed, managed and administered one of the most important social welfare institutions in the region. The LBS's female volunteers contributed their own time and money, canvassed for funds, and provided outdoor relief to the sick and destitute, including a soup kitchen. In 1848, the LBS began operating a day school and orphan asylum. Although the day school was closed in 1853, the work of the Hamilton Orphan Asylum and Ladies' Benevolent Society (HOA/LBS), as the association was renamed in 1852, carried on. In 1875, the HOA/LBS added an Aged Women's Home (AWH) to their enterprises. By the early 1890s, admissions to the orphan asylum were in steady decline, as other kinds of childcare models were developed, and this branch of work was eventually abandoned in 1914. The AWH continued to provide residential care for elderly women; in 1958, the Aged Women's Home was renamed Idlewyld Manor, which exists to this day as a long-term care facility for seniors.[4]

This case study relies principally on the HOA/LBS's voluminous and meticulously kept records. For the entirety of its institutional history, the association's activities were recorded in the minutes of monthly and bi-monthly meetings. Volunteer members, designated as "visitors," were obligated to submit reports at regular meetings about the aid they distributed in their wards, and these too have been preserved. Visitors who were assigned to oversee the affairs of the Orphan Asylum and later the Aged Women's Home also submitted reports that were kept in the minute books. The HOA/LBS published annual reports that presented the association's accomplishments, challenges, and financial statements to the general public. These sources provide the basis for a richly detailed institutional history.

This book's aims are more ambitious, however. *Private Women and the Public Good* is a micro-historical analysis that creates an aperture through which transnational phenomena can be glimpsed. Since this book's central focus is a women's association, gender themes of course run throughout. The HOA/LBS's history is also interwoven with other processes that evolved in Canada and elsewhere over the course of the nineteenth century: the emergence of a public sphere, transplantation of liberal political ideologies, and state formation. While its institutional and geographical focus is narrow, the book's themes are not.

The principal contribution this study makes is to the historiography of female voluntary associationalism. British, American, and Canadian historians have identified scores of voluntary associations in which nineteenth-century women were involved, and this has spawned a similarly large number of interpretations about their meaning and significance. These interpretations have been largely dominated by debates about "separate spheres." In 1974, anthropologist Michelle Rosaldo argued that women's status was lowest in societies where women's and men's spheres of influence were most separate and rigidly defined. According to Rosaldo, women could improve their status in these societies either by entering men's domain or creating a supportive and empowering women's culture separate from men.[5] The twin notions that women's relegation to a separate sphere was the source of her unequal status in society and that women could resist this marginalization provided women's historians with a framework for studying women as active agents capable of challenging patriarchy.

For second-wave feminists writing in the 1970s and 1980s, nineteenth-century women's involvement in charity, moral, and social reform associations seemed to fulfill the promise of separate spheres: these women expanded their spheres of influence beyond the domestic realm and created a supportive female culture that could stimulate a sense of shared oppression and ultimately lead to agitation for political rights.[6] The idea that an empowering women's culture developed out of associationalism was, however, challenged later by historians who argued that divisions between and among women in associations along class, racial, and religious lines undermined any possibility of female solidarity. These women, who were primarily white, middle-class, evangelical Protestants, tended not to challenge status quo inequalities, and only rarely did their activism in associations lead to feminist political engagement.[7]

In the late 1980s and 1990s, the separate spheres paradigm was challenged on another front; namely, men's and women's spheres were rhetorical constructions that did not accurately describe lived experiences.

Feminist historians were enjoined to resist reifying dichotomous spheres, turn their attention away from women's domestic activities, and look for women's activities in other domains.[8] The history of nineteenth-century associationalism offered up numerous examples of white, middle-class, evangelical Protestant women in extra-domestic settings. Charity, moral, and social reform work took women volunteers out onto the streets, into general meeting places, and put their activities onto the pages of the press and governments' agendas. The general conclusion of these studies has been that voluntary associationalism empowered the women involved and provided opportunities for politicization because it gave them access to the "public sphere."[9] The public sphere, according to these analyses, refers to extra-domestic spaces that, it has been assumed, were available for political appropriation by marginal social groups.

This interpretation is problematic in several ways. First, the public sphere as it is deployed in these studies simply reconstitutes the basic premise of the separate spheres paradigm, which is that women's activities outside the domestic sphere ipso facto challenged asymmetrical gender relations. It therefore ignores a more significant critique that separate spheres were epiphenomena of other social, political, and discursive processes that functioned to organize Victorians' worlds in particular ways, which need to be explained and understood.[10] The argument that separate spheres was merely a rhetorical construction and thus easily countered by women's acts also fails to account for the power that the discourses that divided the world between men and women, public and private had for Victorians. Lastly, to assume that the public sphere was formally egalitarian ignores the complexity of the political meanings attached to "publicness," as well as their social consequences.

I argue here that the social, political, and discursive processes that gave meaning and power to the ideology of separate spheres effectively contained the political implications of associational women's activities despite their agency. This case study also shows that divisions between public and private spheres were fundamental to protecting particular interests at the expense of others. Upholding these distinctions was essential to maintaining the inequalities that many Victorians believed provided stability and order in their society. Using Jürgen Habermas's explication in *The Structural Transformation of the Public Sphere,* I contend that the public sphere functioned to consolidate rather than mitigate asymmetrical social and political relations in the nineteenth century.

Habermas's interpretation of the public sphere is pertinent to a feminist analysis of separate spheres, in general, and an examination of women's charitable associationalism in nineteenth-century Hamilton, in particular, because it offers a systematic analysis of the political and ideological bases of the private/public division in Western societies. Habermas's work, which has been the subject of considerable debate amongst feminists,[11] has also been misappropriated to substantiate the claim that nineteenth-century associations provided women with access to the public sphere.[12]

According to Habermas, the public sphere was a historical phenomenon that evolved out of a confluence of liberal political philosophy, laissez-faire capitalism, and a proliferation of print culture in the post-Enlightenment West. The public sphere was neither a place nor space, as some have argued, but rather a discursive process whereby issues of common concern were debated by members of civil society. According to liberal theory, these debates ideally generated a rational consensus that was designated as "public opinion." In this context, public opinion came to be regarded as a legitimate expression of political will that ought to be brought to bear upon civic affairs.[13]

The function of the political public sphere, according to Habermas, was to subject domination – by the state or other interest groups – to "standards of reason."[14] In theory, only the rationality of arguments rather than the subjective identity of speakers ought to influence public opinion and affect decisions about issues of common concern.[15] Therefore, no one person's or group's interests could dominate public opinion because only those whose rational arguments passed the test of public debate could represent themselves as "the public."[16] This was not a process whereby marginal interest groups could articulate their political concerns. On the contrary, the modus operandi of the public sphere was to "overcome particular social expression."[17]

An argument, for example, that a particular civic arrangement ought to be endorsed because it benefited women, politically or otherwise, would be disregarded as subjective, interested, and particular.[18] Any attempt to represent women's interests qua women would vitiate claims to speak on behalf of the public and therefore lack legitimacy in debates that constituted the public sphere. Of course, claims made by men that shored up masculine political privileges were not perceived as subjective or interested since the universal political subject of liberal political theory was embodied as male.[19]

Women were excluded from participation in a political public sphere on other grounds as well. Habermas goes on to explain that in spite of the premise that the public sphere was inclusive and therefore theoretically accessible to anyone who could articulate rational arguments, in practice, participation was possible only for those whose education and property ownership qualified them as citizens.[20] According to liberal theory, the public sphere's principle of inclusivity was not threatened insofar as everyone had an equal opportunity to become a property owner and educated. "If," Habermas writes, "everyone ... had a chance to become a 'citizen,' then only citizens should be allowed into the political public sphere, without this restriction amounting to an abandonment of the principle of publicity."[21]

Lack of access to property was a significant political barrier for women in British North America. Property ownership was the sine qua non of nineteenth-century liberal citizenship, and individuals without property were believed to lack both a stake in society and a legitimate interest in the public good. In other words, only property owners' private interests (protection of property) converged with the common interest (protection of the property order).[22] Also, according to liberal ideology, only property owners were at liberty to exercise their political duties according to conscience rather than compulsion. The dependence of women, children, and slaves, who relied on others for their livelihood and could therefore easily be coerced, was a foil to property-owning men's independent status.[23]

During the nineteenth century, most women in Canada West/Ontario were the legal dependants of their husbands or fathers. Since wives generally lacked rights to property brought into or acquired after their marriage as long as their husband was alive until 1872, most women lacked the right to participate in politics and, therefore, the political public sphere.[24] Property-owning widows sometimes slipped through a legal loophole and exercised their vote, until provincial legislatures amended the franchise laws during the 1830s and 1840s and specified that only *male* property owners had this right of citizenship.[25]

Even if we were to concede the tendentious claim that everyone had equal access to an education and property, clearly not everyone had a chance to become a man. Women's exclusion from the political public sphere was rooted in a liberal political ideology that insisted that maleness was fundamental to political belonging.

The challenges that ultimately prevented HOA/LBS women from leveraging their charitable activities into an effective resistance to their subordinate status is perhaps most clear in comparisons between how these women represented their work in annual reports (Chapter 2) and how they were represented in public debates by men who were deemed capable of speaking on behalf of the public (Chapter 4). Although HOA/LBS annual reports avoided rhetoric that called attention to the managers' particularity as women and instead invoked gender-neutral language to make claims on behalf of a "Christian public," women were powerless to resist particular property-owning men's representation of their work as "natural" to their sex, politically benign, and fundamentally private in the debates that constituted the public sphere.

Feminist historians' commitment to a narrative of women's progressive incorporation into liberal society through their active agency has led them to ignore what is perhaps most fascinating about Habermas's explanation, which is that despite the public sphere's superficial basis in egalitarian rhetoric, it functioned to transform property-owning men's interests into a nominally legitimate consensus (public opinion) whilst excluding competing interest groups from debates about common concerns. In other words, the public sphere was instrumental in the negotiation of hegemonic social relations.

That the public sphere functioned in this way opens up other analytical possibilities – namely, an examination of its interconnectedness with an evolving liberal project of rule in nineteenth-century British North America. This is a second historiographical issue with which this study engages. In his 2000 article, "The Liberal Order Framework," Ian McKay invited historians of Canada to study the introduction, transplantation, and transformation of "a certain politico-economic logic," which can be broadly defined as liberalism, on political practice and public discourse.[26] While liberalism's central premises are relatively stable and thus identifiable, the specific variants that liberal practices took in particular times and places were highly contingent. Therefore, the study of political ideology and cultural transformation can be brought together to explore the unique historical forms into which liberalism evolved in northern North America.

McKay contends that liberalism's most fundamental tenet is "a belief in the epistemological and ontological primacy of the category 'individual.'"[27] The notion that the individual is prior to and therefore ought to be served by society rather than vice versa is liberalism's first principle. A logical sequence follows from this first principle, which is composed of three elementary parts: liberty, equality, and property.[28] A liberal order arranges these parts hierarchically. Property, specifically an individual's right to own property freehold, is of first-order importance, and indeed both liberty and equality are impossible to achieve without it. Liberty is defined largely in relationship to property, that is, individual freedom from constraint to dispose of and use private property. Equality in liberal terms refers not to equality of station but rather equality of opportunity. Liberal discourses of equality were meant to empower men of so-called talent and virtue rather than high birth. These fundamentals are the basis upon which the panoply of other liberal precepts is built.

The public sphere's theoretical basis in liberal philosophy is evinced in the premises that "man" is capable of rationality, consensus arises out of rational debate, civil society is composed of citizens coming together as equals, and so forth. In terms of praxis, its rootedness in liberal ideology is clear: the public sphere operated as a discursive process whereby property-owning men's prerogatives to define the public good were legitimated, contested, and, ultimately, normalized. Thus, studying the public sphere can illuminate how liberalism's central principles, as well as its more amorphous elements, were implanted, adjusted to local conditions, and affected social and political relationships.

In Hamilton's case, ethnoreligious identity was centrally important to the operation of political power dynamics within a liberal public sphere. Notwithstanding liberal precepts that equated separation of church and state with liberty of conscience, and despite considerable lip service paid to the importance of nonsectarianism in public affairs, Roman Catholic property owners were not accorded equal status in debates that constituted the public sphere. Nor did they share equally in the disbursement of power or privileges by the local state. This is particularly clear in debates about the distribution of public funding to charitable institutions in Hamilton at mid-century (Chapter 4).

Protestant men used their formal and informal power, within the city council and in the realm of public opinion, to protect public funding for the HOA/LBS, which was, despite claims to the contrary, a sectarian institution. This is an example of how interrogating the particulars of liberal governance can reveal its historical variants: the context of large-scale Irish Roman Catholic migration to Canada West during the 1840s created fractures within the category of liberal citizen along ethnoreligious lines. These fractures had very real consequences for how, to whom, and under what conditions both charity and power were distributed in Hamilton.

A third historiographical contribution that this study makes is to the history of state formation, in particular by considering its connectedness to the public sphere and an evolving liberal order. State formation scholars have identified a progressive enlargement of state apparatuses and a concomitant expansion of its capacity to regulate and intervene into the everyday lives of the populous especially during the modern era. This is significant insofar as particular sets of values were able to be promulgated somewhat more systematically and effectively than had been the case previously. State formation facilitated a process of moral regulation whereby state and state-sanctioned bodies could, through both legitimation and discipline, circumscribe the extent to which individuals and groups could either conceptualize or act out political, social, and economic alternatives.[29]

The process of state formation is particularly relevant to the provision of charity in Canada West. In Britain and those parts of British North America where the Poor Laws were enacted, the connections between the state and charity are fairly clear. In their absence, as in the case of Upper Canada/Canada West, charity was nonetheless rarely left to private initiative entirely, despite the impression that the state was uninvolved. Political rhetoric that insisted that voluntary initiative was superior to public social welfare programs helped create the illusion that charities actually operated autonomously from the state.[30]

Whether its intervention came in the form of direct subsidies or in the provision of laws governing charities, the state facilitated a coordination of its representatives' and constituents' interests with charitable institutions capable of embodying those interests. Moreover, property-owning men's prerogative to define the public good, according to a shifting set of liberal principles, and their capacity to speak on behalf of the public and marshal public opinion in support of their definition, also could and did affect the extent and nature of both private and state support for charitable endeavours.

The case of charitable provision in mid-nineteenth-century Hamilton bears these general principles out. The HOA/LBS's success or failure depended on its capacity to calibrate its work to the interests represented by the local state and to secure favourable public opinion. Its attempts to do so (Chapter 2) and its partnership with the Hamilton City Council (Chapter 3) show how extensive the connections were among private charity, the state, and the public sphere. The difficulties that the association faced when its claims to serve the public good were challenged (Chapter 4) illustrate how state sanction and the particular constitution of the public sphere worked to legitimate the claims of Protestant property-owning men and marginalized, denigrated, or ignored the interests of Roman Catholic property owners, women, and non-property owners.

Private charities such as the HOA/LBS also operated within an Act of Incorporation, which was a legal mechanism that, once assented to by the provincial parliament, transformed an association of individuals, in this case, a male board of trustees, into a single legal individual, capable of holding property, suing and being sued, signing contracts, and so on. This state sanction protected "actual" individuals from suits and other claims on personal property for debts or liabilities incurred by the association. Incorporation also granted legal powers to pursue particular ends, along with certain conditions that made it accountable to the state and/or its stakeholders.[31]

In the case of charities that involved dependent children, acts of incorporation delegated state power to committees of management, often composed of women, that enabled them to abrogate parental rights to any child in the care of the institution and, therefore, empowered these committees to intervene into private life to a degree that has not been widely acknowledged by historians (Chapter 5). These prerogatives were, however, subordinated to the authority of male trustees and conditional upon making the association's management and financial affairs available to public scrutiny. By granting or not granting acts of incorporation, the state could regulate putatively private charitable institutions and thereby empower those that served the so-called public good while leaving ultimate control to particular interest groups, in this case, property-owning Protestant men.

A final historiographical theme addressed here relates to the study of children and childhood. Generally speaking, late-nineteenth-century developments in the regulation and administration of children and families by the state, reformers, and experts have dominated English Canadian scholarship. A plethora of evidence about the 1880 to 1920 era, more than a dearth of evidence about the 1840 to 1875 period, could leave the impression that the advent of the "modern" child was a late-century phenomenon.[32] Several studies have identified shifts during the mid-nineteenth century toward regarding children as emotional rather than economic assets, as innocent and susceptible to influence, and in need of specialized care.[33] The idea that state intervention into intact families and the doctrine of "the best interest of the child" were late-century phenomena has, however, gone largely unchallenged.

The case of the Hamilton Orphan Asylum provides additional evidence that considerable continuity existed in child welfare practices and ideologies from the mid-nineteenth century to the beginning of the twentieth century. The techniques used by the Committee of Management to care for children – namely, institutional care, apprenticeship, and adoption – reflected typically modern notions about children and childhood (Chapter 6). A principle of environmentalism that assumed children were naturally innocent prevailed. Institutional care was used only when children could not be placed back into their own homes or provided with a substitute home. Managers expected that children ought to have opportunities for play and work, religious and academic education, as well as training, and to receive both affection and discipline.

Although the technique of apprenticing children took for granted their economic value, the HOA managers devised policies and strategies to guard children, especially young children, against economic exploitation and to ensure decent treatment, an education, and at least some financial compensation for their labour. Adoption, in contrast to apprenticing, was treated as a strictly affective relationship based on an expectation that non-biological children could and should be raised by parents as if the child was "their own." It is important to remember that these were ideal scenarios. Perhaps children in the HOA's care actually experienced and benefited from these arrangements; surely some did not.

The asylum's cooperative relationship with Hamilton City Council and its Act of Incorporation, as mentioned above, show that precedents for interventions into parental rights and state support for child welfare institutions were established by the 1850s. The local and provincial state implicitly or explicitly delegated its powers of *parens patriae* to the HOA's Committee of Management, who then could and did choose either to preserve parental rights or to act in a child's apparent best interest according to its own judgment (Chapter 5). During the last quarter of the nineteenth century, undeniably, the degree of state involvement increased and its powers enlarged significantly. Intervention techniques and modes of regulation were not however created ex nihilo. Nor were child savers' and reformers' practices and principles as innovative and revolutionary as they claimed (Chapter 7).

Private Women and the Public Good travels over varied ground: politics, gender, charity, the state, religion, civil society, childhood. These are linked by locale (Hamilton) and institutional focus (HOA/LBS). A conceptual framework also binds these elements together. This framework asserts that a discursively constituted public sphere, an evolving liberal order, and an ongoing process of state formation were interwoven in complex ways. The results of setting these elements – politics, gender, charity, and so on – into this framework demonstrates the fundamental interconnectedness of ideas and experiences.

1
Hamilton, Upper Canada, to 1846

HISTORICAL EVENTS THAT preceded the LBS's establishment in 1846 are crucial to an understanding of this association and its wider context. Hamilton's early development, on the one hand, mirrored that of other towns and cities in frontier regions of northern North America. On the other, the specific timing, extent, and circumstances of that development were in some ways unique.[1] This chapter knits together a historical narrative made of threads pulled from continental, provincial, and local histories. It also introduces the personal history of Lydia Jackson, who was a founding member of the LBS and served on its executive until her death in 1875. Precious few remnants exist to tell us anything about the lives of the women who founded and built this association. Jackson is, however, an exception in this regard. At her death, Nathanael Burwash, a Methodist minister and the dean of theology at Victoria College, wrote and published her eulogy. A narrative of her early life, which begins this chapter, is interwoven with larger historical processes and leads into an examination of how liberal state formation and the emergence of a political public sphere enabled a particular group of men to exercise control over formal and informal mechanisms of power, which ultimately empowered the LBS to undertake its work.

Lydia Sanford's family did not wholeheartedly approve of her decision, at the age of twenty-two, to marry Edward Jackson. Lydia, who was born in 1804 in Redding, Connecticut, had lost her mother as a young girl and had no sisters to guide or counsel her. Edward was an apprentice tinsmith and his family had neither wealth nor status. Perhaps worse, especially in the eyes of Lydia's extremely devout Methodist father, his family was Episcopalian. Edward was handsome and gregarious, had a great sense of humour, and, apparently, "did not altogether escape the dangers and temptations to which such qualities expose a young man."[2] Lydia's family likely recognized that her choice in marriage was the single most important decision she would make in life.

Once married, Lydia would have few other opportunities to make independent decisions. According to the law of *feme covert* in effect in both the United States and British North America, her legal existence would cease at the moment of her marriage. Any financial assets she might have held or would hold in the future, as well as any wages she might earn, would become her husband's property to dispose of as he wished. She would be very unlikely to be granted a legal divorce unless she could prove that his physical abuse threatened her life. She would have no parental authority over any children from the marriage even in the event of his death, unless Edward specifically designated her as their guardian in his will. Her well-being would be almost entirely dependent on whether Edward could support her financially, if he chose to treat her with kindness, and whether or not he exercised good judgment in his private and public affairs.

Soon after their marriage in 1826, Lydia and Edward moved west. Pressure on Edward to launch himself as an independent man likely hastened the couple's migration away from Connecticut. The Jacksons followed what was in those years a veritable exodus by migrants from the settled parts of the United States into western frontiers in Ohio, Illinois, Michigan, and Canada. The couple landed in Niagara, Upper Canada, with some household furniture, a few tinsmithing tools, and little more, since they had exhausted their funds on the journey itself. Edward sold some of their furniture and borrowed a hundred dollars to purchase stock and set up his shop.

Within fifteen months of settling in Niagara, Edward repaid his debt, accumulated a little cash, and decided to move Lydia and their household again to Ancaster. This move was followed shortly after by another, ultimately permanent one to Hamilton in 1832.[3] At that time, Hamilton was a burgeoning village. In 1816, George Hamilton, who was the son of prominent Queenston merchant Robert Hamilton, had used his government connections to get the Gore District courthouse built on a piece of his land that lay between the Niagara Escarpment and Burlington Bay. He had also granted adjacent land for a market and a town site. The courthouse, which also served as the district's administrative centre, generated some collateral economic activity.[4]

Hamilton's early development, like that of Upper Canada more generally, was dependent most on the settlement of its agricultural frontier. In addition to westward migrants like the Jacksons from the United States, who were compelled by mounting pressure on available land to seek opportunities elsewhere, immigrants from Britain flowed into Upper and Lower Canada after the end of the Napoleonic wars. By the 1820s, farm families that had moved into the area began to produce surpluses that they sold to local merchants for goods in kind, credit, or, less often, cash. Merchants were integral to the development of markets for locally produced products as well as access to items that farm families could not or opted not to produce themselves.[5]

The town's economic growth was also fuelled by the Burlington Canal project that was a joint private-public venture completed in 1827, which traversed a sandy spit of land that cut Hamilton off from direct access to Lake Ontario. The Jacksons' move from Ancaster to Hamilton was a response to the significant improvement this project had on the latter town's access to the people and goods that flowed into and out of the Great Lakes region. Edward purchased a town lot and set up a tinsmith shop with two partners in 1831. By 1832, the Hamilton Tin Factory employed at least five men.[6]

The canal exposed Hamilton to more than just people and products. Contact with the outside world also brought disease. In 1831-32, most of British North America was swept by a cholera epidemic from which Hamilton was not spared.[7] Since the causes of this disease were little known, cholera visited both death and fear upon Upper Canadians. Immigrants, who had theretofore been welcomed as economic assets, were singled out as harbingers of the disease and were quarantined in sheds on the waterfront.[8]

A local religious revival followed in the wake of the cholera epidemic in Hamilton. The town's first church, a Methodist chapel, had been built in 1824. During the revival, Methodist preachers James Evans and Edwy Ryerson made converts out of as many as one hundred Hamiltonians, which represented nearly one out of every six residents.[9] In rural areas in Upper Canada throughout the 1820s and 1830s, evangelical enthusiasm stimulated revivals such as this one that awakened religious fervour in some and recommitted others to their faith. Lydia and Edward Jackson, as well as his apprentices and employees, were amongst the converts.

Although early nineteenth-century revivals evoked a spirit of emotionalism and intense individual experience that contrasted starkly with the orderly decorum of established churches, by the 1830s, Methodist evangelicals were intent upon moving their sect into the religious and cultural mainstream. Evangelicals began to stress that conversion was but a first step toward complete rededication of one's life to God. Backsliding was a great threat that had to be overcome by constant self-examination and active involvement in a host of church- and extra–church-related activities.[10] Upon joining the Methodist congregation, Edward paid off the parsonage's $600 debt and began leading weekly class meetings and prayer sessions in his and Lydia's home.[11]

Hamilton's economy was booming. After the canal's completion, the number of houses in the town doubled and its three stores multiplied to eighteen. In 1833, the town's population was 1,400, and its port was served by four steamboats as well as a stagecoach.[12] In the same year, a board of police was established, which was a partially elected body with the authority to appoint functionaries, such as pound keepers or tax assessors, and to set regulatory practices like tavern licensing and fire prevention.[13] Edward Jackson served on the board in 1837-38. According to an 1834 newspaper report in the *Western Mercury,* during a recent but unspecified period four hundred town lots had been sold.[14] In 1835, the town's size had almost doubled to 2,600.[15]

Between 1830 and 1842, the population of the Gore District tripled, due in large part to an influx of about eighteen thousand immigrants.[16] Migrants who came to Canada either as farm labourers or later as workers on large-scale construction projects likely hoped to eventually launch themselves as independent land holders. Rising costs of land and low wages thwarted the ambitions of many immigrant workers.[17] Internal migrations led men and women with only their labour to sell into towns and cities such as Hamilton.

Despite local commentators' convictions that, in Upper Canada, "honest industry can never want employment," cyclical or seasonal fluctuations in labour demands as well as personal crises such as illness, injury, or death could easily thrust recent immigrants and labourers into acute economic straits.[18] No formal state provisions had been made for coping with destitute individuals, so responsibility for poor relief most often fell to churches or private individuals and less often to magistrates and local governments.[19] In Hamilton, the Board of Police provided aid in desperate cases to "paupers" in the form of tax relief, payment for medical care, board, travel expenses, funeral costs, or direct pecuniary aid. Assistance was doled out in meagre amounts. According to the Board of Police minutes, between September 1840 and April 1846, only eleven individuals had been assisted.[20]

In this period Hamilton, like many other towns in Upper Canada, was experiencing significant economic transformation from a "market place" to a "market economy."[21] As the Gore District hinterland began to fill up and material surpluses accumulated on frontier farms, merchants capitalized on opportunities to purchase raw goods, which they would in turn sell locally or export to larger markets.[22] These businessmen also supplied farm families with cash or credit and access to a relatively wide array of imported and manufactured goods.[23] As early as the 1830s, local prices began to converge with those of large markets such as New York and Montreal. Additional evidence from newspaper reports suggests that buyers and sellers in Hamilton had begun to adopt an objective cash standard that was disembedded from local conditions.[24]

During the 1840s, in the aftermath of the Rebellions and Lord Durham's report, more political power in Upper Canada slowly began to devolve to elected representatives, and greater numbers of property-owning men were able to participate in governance than had been previously the case. More representative government did not, however, lead to the wholesale replacement of local oligarchies and patronage appointees. As Bruce Curtis has argued, these political changes simply "modif[ied] the conditions under which they could rule."[25] The radical potential of democratic processes was counteracted by an expanding state system that was able to intervene into daily life. New departments, bureaucracies, and inspectors diffused the emergent state's regulatory power. The creation of municipal councils and city corporations with more powers of appointment, administration, and taxation also facilitated a coordination of central–local government relations.[26]

Coextensive with the growth of the state's institutional apparatus was a legitimizing project that sought to reshape individual and collective behaviours. Public schooling, introduced in Canada West in 1846, was particularly important for its role in teaching the citizenry "its 'rights and duties.'" These included "respect for the practical limits to democratic government imposed by allowing men of property to speak for society as a whole" and guardianship over "the inequitable distribution of property, of women's subordination, and of the dominance of the 'white' races."[27] In other words, schooling was essential to the process of moral regulation, whereby capitalism, liberalism, patriarchy, and white supremacy were normalized.

Just as public schooling was a forum for inculcating particular values deemed essential to the proper operation of democracy, so too were voluntary associations and the press. Jeffrey McNairn explains that in Upper Canada voluntary associations like Freemasonry, Temperance

Societies, and Mechanics' Institutes were schools for "democratic sociability."[28] In associations, men developed skills and knowledge for rational argument and critical debate, which were essential to political participation in democratic society. Associations were also "mini-republics"; members' consent created a body that was self-governing and members tacitly agreed to obey rules and policies imposed by the group.[29] Members entered into associations as individuals and equals, each expected to have a voice in the association, and officers were elected from the ranks on the basis of their peers' favourable judgment. McNairn shows that "by generalizing these skills and expectations, voluntary associations encourage[d] participants to reproduce them elsewhere."[30] In other words, associational life was a specific form of liberal democracy writ small that provided certain men with opportunities to act out and become accustomed to political roles.

Despite his emphasis on the democratizing effects of a liberal public sphere, McNairn's analysis of Upper Canadian politics also shows how voluntary associations and the press worked to preserve status quo inequalities in a period of potentially more substantive political change. These institutions, according to McNairn, "diffused the norms and mechanisms of the public sphere, in part, by differentiating them from alternatives." These institutions also "differentiated those deemed capable of participating from those who weren't."[31] This latter category included the poor, "immature" or immoral men, and women.

By the 1840s, a number of all-male voluntary associations had been established in Hamilton, including a Freemasons' and Oddfellows' Lodge, as well as a Highland Society and a St. Andrew's, St. George's, and St. Patrick's Society. Religious and humanitarian associations, such as a Church Society, Temperance Society, and Abolition Society, had been founded, as well as autodidactic institutions such as the Mechanics' Institute, Mercantile Library Association, Literary Society, and Young Men's Debating Club. These associations gave property-owning men like Edward Jackson opportunities to socialize, self-educate, engage in charity and mutual assistance, and discuss and debate topics of common concern.

Like associations, the press was a feature of civil society that was essential to the development of a political public sphere. Certainly, democracy required informed citizens and a free press. Newspaper reading also provided men with an opportunity to imagine themselves as individuals within a larger, self-selected community. Rhetorical appeals to "the public" in advertisements and editorials in papers consolidated men's sense of belonging and prerogative to participate in debate and discussion. Also, arguments made in newspaper forums elided the author's particular identity, which encouraged readers to judge arguments on the basis of rationality and logic rather than personal status or influence. Divergent opinions set out by flagrantly partisan editors, oftentimes in direct conversation with one another, also introduced readers to debating techniques and norms, as well as opportunities to exercise their judgment and weigh choices.[32]

In the mid-1840s, at least four newspapers had been established in Hamilton. The *Hamilton Express* was a Reform party paper started in 1836 by an Irish Protestant Orangeman named Solomon Brega. This paper was subsequently absorbed by an existing Reform paper, *Hamilton Journal and Gore District Mercantile and Agricultural Intelligencer* and published after 1835 by Edward Cartwright Thomas as the *Journal and Express.*[33] George Perkins Bull, an Anglican and committed Orangeman, published the moderate Conservative paper *Hamilton Gazette* beginning in 1834.[34] In July 1846, Robert Smiley was reputedly invited by Hamilton businessmen to "give voice and leadership" to the conservative cause and began publishing and editing the *Hamilton Spectator.*[35]

In 1846, on the eve of its incorporation as a city, Hamilton was home to nearly seven thousand residents. By this time, a well-established group of men held a near monopoly on the roles and responsibilities of civic government and civil society. Michael Doucet and John Weaver argue that, by the 1840s, a cohort of property owners was "able to identify common interests and to pursue development policy."[36] These men "jointly promoted the town ... endorsed and circulated each others [sic] promissory notes, and generally guided the town's economic and physical development."[37] According to Weaver, Hamilton's local oligarchy "acted with a measure of public sanction because their interest in community expansion with its promise of jobs could be embraced by all social groups."[38] Entrepreneurial men received government support because their projects were regarded to be "in the public interest, serving the community."[39]

Hamilton's Municipal Act of Incorporation, put into force by its passage in the provincial legislature in June 1846, institutionalized the political dominance of men of property, entrenched their property rights, and empowered an elected body to stimulate capitalist development and regulate social order. The act represented a partial devolution of power from appointed magistrates and district councils to locally elected officials. Hamilton's incorporation was, however, also part of a politico-philosophical and cultural transformation wherein property-owning men were vested with power by the provincial state over taxation, administration, and economic development, as well as the prosecution and protection of others.[40]

The negotiation of political power within debates that constituted the public sphere is evinced in local newspaper accounts leading up to Hamilton's first municipal election. The *Spectator* reported on one of Hamilton's first council nomination meetings, which was held in early October 1846. In this instance, property-owning men's existing political power was shored up by an unidentified writer who wielded discourses of proper public comportment and manliness at a crucial moment when Hamilton's municipal powers were structurally democratized.

According to the author, bad behaviour and rowdiness prevailed at a nomination meeting in St. Andrew's ward prior to Hamilton's first city election. These actions, he proposed, "may do well enough for an hour's frolic" but were "scarcely the thing that is expected from a public meeting." The report described a "heterogeneous mass of men, boys, dogs and broken benches" and "some half dozen acting on the principle that they have as good a right to speak as anyone else." The writer regarded this meeting's "heterogeneity" as evidence of disorder. He disparaged these men's masculinity – and thereby their political legitimacy – by associating them with "boys, [and] dogs." The attendees' physicality (evinced by broken furniture) and impudence (evinced by their refusal to defer to others) are also clearly troublesome to the writer. In contrast, the "gentlemen" at the meeting addressed the crowd with decorum and reputedly behaved themselves in a way that was more "creditable to the city."[41] Challengers to existing power relations, who did not allow "gentlemen" to speak for them, were discredited in the report, and Hamiltonians were persuaded to support only those candidates who already conformed to a particular standard of comportment in public forums.

In December of the same year, the *Spectator* published a letter addressed to "the Electors of the City of Hamilton" that offered a dire warning. The author, "a Voter," reminded his audience that they had "an important duty" on voting day. He insisted that "it is absolutely necessary that you elect men known for their intelligence and who command the respect of the community." Only these men could be trusted with "the judicious management of a large revenue." The "character" of Hamilton's councillors would determine whether or not "necessary loans for the improvement of the city" would be obtained.[42] Again in January 1847, ten days prior to Hamilton's first municipal election, another *Spectator* editorial sent the same basic message. The author reminded voters of the "absolute necessity for selecting as councillors the men on whom they can faithfully rely." If "by an improper selection of councillors we show persons at a distance that we are careless in the management of our internal affairs, we cannot expect capitalists to repose confidence in either the city corporation, or those who established it."[43]

These reports betray anxiety about the democratic process and an effort to ensure some protection of existing power relations. Men of intelligence, character, reliability, and respectability were particularly designated as more capable of judging the best interests of the community than others. These authors also tied political legitimacy to the ability to foster capitalist development, which attempted to consolidate the political prerogatives of those in whom investors would "repose confidence." These discourses illustrate clearly that the press functioned as both a discursive site for debates that constituted the political public sphere and a forum for the organization of consent to a particular political and economic order.

After the elections, the *Spectator* "happily" reported that the voting "went off quietly and peaceably." The author expressed "great satisfaction at the manner in which the electors performed their duty."[44] The voters had indeed entrusted authority to those who already possessed power and influence. For example, Colin Campbell Ferrie, who was the director of the Gore Bank, which underwrote the city's first operating loan, was elected in St. Mary's ward and appointed mayor.[45] St. Andrew's ward, whose notoriously rowdy nomination meeting had been reported upon in October, elected John Willson. Willson had been a resident since the early part of the century and a former (appointed) justice of the peace and surrogate judge for the Gore District. He had also been elected to Upper Canada's House of Assembly.[46]

These men and those like them would continue to take on leadership roles in Hamilton during the 1850s and 1860s. In his analysis of the 1851 and 1861 census data, Michael Katz identified approximately 161 men who held a disproportionately large proportion of Hamilton's total property, wealth, and political power. These men were prominent in the trades and business, included merchants, proprietors, manufacturers, and professionals, and promoted social and educational life in the city. They shared social, familial, and associational ties, and they were nearly all Protestants.[47]

According to Katz, these men "made the public interests of Hamilton and their private economic prospects the same" and "their promotion of railroads, utilities, and schools undoubtedly reflected their perception of the contribution these modern innovations would make to the general prosperity of their city and their own fortunes." They shared common interests, "were capable of defending those interests when they perceived them threatened," and "exerted enormous influence over the commercial, political, and associational life" of Hamilton.[48] These men constituted a particularly influential cohort with direct involvement in various state or state-sanctioned institutions and unrestricted access to the political public sphere.

These men's values and behaviours were generally consistent with cultural attributes of "the middle class" in other parts of the trans-Atlantic world. This cohort was not, however, merely an economic class. For example, as Chapter 4 will demonstrate more clearly, they allied against relatively wealthy, property-owning men who were not Anglo-Protestants. Although they were hardly egalitarian, many of their values, if not always their interests, were shared by much less wealthy members of the community. Indeed, these men's ability to surpass the limits of their own interests and speak on behalf of the public in simple "common sense" ways was crucial to maintaining their leadership roles in this community. Although the term *middle class* is a convenient label with which to identify this group, these Hamiltonians ought to be considered, more precisely, as a white, male, Protestant, propertied interest group.

The women who played key roles in the LBS were, not surprisingly, the female kin of this interest group's members. By cross-referencing the data from LBS minute books with local histories, the occupational status of forty-one of fifty-eight members who served during the LBS's first year of operations can be identified. The close male kin of all these women were professionals, such as doctors, lawyers, and military officers, or businessmen, merchants, bankers, or manufacturers.[49] These findings are consistent with those of Haley Bamman, who collated LBS membership data from 1851-52 and 1861-62 and cross-referenced it with census and assessment records for 1851 and 1861. Bamman found that the Ladies' Benevolent Society was "composed of women of high-status, both economic and social, and who ruled over fairly large households." While Bamman admits that the LBS was not monolithic, "the parameters for acceptance within the Society were too narrow to include any but the wealthiest of the skilled trades – certainly no lower."[50]

The following series of biographical sketches give a partial glimpse into the lives of women about whom we otherwise know almost nothing. Their biographies are meant to briefly foreground the experiences of a few individuals who played key roles in this association but, since no personal papers are extant, tend to recede into the background in this analysis. These sketches are also meant to show the dense network of familial, associational, occupational, and denominational connections amongst these women and their male kin.

Elizabeth Caddy Thomas was chosen to be the LBS's first president, which was a position she maintained for twenty-nine years. She had at least three daughters and was married to Edward Cartwright Thomas. Cartwright Thomas first appears in Hamilton history at the age of thirty-three as the editor of the Reform newspaper, the *Journal and Express,* and then a clerk of the Gore District Council. In 1841, he was appointed sheriff of Wentworth County. When the Mechanics' Institute was founded in 1839 he served as vice president. He also served on St. George's Benevolent Society's first Charitable Committee in 1843 and was a member of the Anglican Church of Ascension.[51] Thomas held a directorship in the Canada Life Assurance Company, which was established in 1847 by Hugh Cossart Baker, whose wife Emma Wyatt was also a founding member of the LBS.

Emma Wyatt Baker was born in England, married in 1845, and raised two sons and four daughters. Her husband, Hugh Baker, an Anglican, had moved to Hamilton in 1843 to manage a branch of the Bank of Montreal. In 1847, he started the first life insurance company in Canada, which was a business venture that was just becoming popular in the United States.[52] The company was established on the joint stock model and subscribed to by Edward Cartwright Thomas as well as John Young, whose wife Anne Coleman was a founding member of the LBS. Both Baker and Young helped found Hamilton's Board of Trade in 1845.

John Young was sent to Hamilton in 1832 by the firm for which he had worked in Montreal and Glasgow to establish a retail dry goods, groceries, and hardware business.[53] He married Anne Coleman in 1835, and they had five children. Young helped establish the Gore Bank in 1836 with the future mayor Colin Ferrie, whose wife Rachel Campbell was a member of the LBS for three years. Young and Ferrie both joined the Mechanics'

Institute in 1839 and the St. Andrew's Benevolent Society when it was established in 1835. Reverend Alexander Gale and William P. McLaren were also founding members of St. Andrew's.

Alexander Gale's wife, Margaret Scarth, was a founding member and vice president of the LBS. She married Gale in 1836 at the age of thirty-three, and they had one son and two daughters, one of whom later joined the LBS. Reverend Gale led his congregation in a split from the Church of Scotland to establish a Free Evangelical Church in 1844.[54]

In 1843, William P. McLaren had married Jane Evatt, who joined the LBS in 1848. McLaren, who emigrated from Scotland and was also a founding member of Hamilton's Board of Trade, established a wholesale grocery firm in 1852.[55] Jane and William were members of the Anglican congregation at the Church of Ascension, along with her two sisters Harriet and Marie, and their husbands Richard Juson and Adam Brown, respectively. The McLarens held bible classes in their home for "poor people who could not go to church." Their mission eventually outgrew the space and was moved to a chapel in Corktown.[56]

Harriet Juson helped found the LBS and served as its accounts secretary until 1867 when she and her husband retired to England. Richard Juson was an English immigrant who set up a hardware business sometime around 1835. He served as a director in Hugh Baker's life insurance company and as a member of the Board of Trade.[57] He was a founding member of the St. George's Benevolent Society and Mechanics' Institute, as was Sheriff Edward C. Thomas and Hugh Baker. Each of these men also joined the Mercantile Library Association along with John Young. When the Church of Ascension broke off from Reverend John Gamble Geddes's congregation at Christ's Church, Juson was the single largest contributor to the building and laid the new church's cornerstone.

John Geddes's wife, Susan Davidson née Stewart, was a founding member of the LBS and served as vice president until 1879 when the couple left Hamilton. They were married in 1842 and had five children. Reverend Geddes came from a Loyalist family and served as curate to Archdeacon George Okill Stuart in Kingston before he was appointed rector of Christ's Church in Hamilton in 1834. Geddes served as chaplain to the jail, hospital, and army, and as headmaster of a local grammar school he started in 1843. Although the Church of Ascension was more evangelical and was reputedly established because "certain members of ... [Geddes's] congregation did not agree with him," this appears not to have negatively affected relations between Susan Geddes and her fellow workers in the LBS who joined the new church.[58]

Lydia Jackson, who served as the LBS's treasurer until her death in 1875, and her husband, Edward, became prominent members of the First Methodist Church. They had three children but only one girl survived childhood. Edward ran a very successful metal works and stove manufacturing business. He was an early director of the Gore Bank, whose other investors include Colin Ferrie and John Young. The Jacksons contributed to church building, missionary, and abolitionist causes, and played instrumental roles in founding the theology department at Victoria College and establishing Hamilton's Wesleyan Female College.[59]

By 1846, large-scale migrations, market revolution, and the slow devolution of power to local governments and elected representatives were beginning to transform Canada West. The promulgation of particular liberal principles, through legislation and political discourse, helped empower a particular cohort of white, Protestant, property-owning men to take up key leadership roles in Hamilton and, to a large extent, define the public good for their community. Their ability to consolidate both legitimated authority and informal influence ultimately empowered their female kin to found and build one of the town's first and most significant charity associations.

2
A "sufficiently extensive and efficient instrumentality"

On May 20, 1846, a group of forty-six women who identified themselves as "the Female members of the several religious congregations" met in Hamilton's Gore District Grammar School. According to their minutes, the meeting's purpose was to establish a Ladies' Benevolent Society, which had as its object "the investigation and relief of cases of distress and destitution arising from sickness, poverty, or similar causes." The minutes justified their actions as follows:

> That there being at all times numerous cases of distress ... requiring the attention and aid of Christian beneficence and no sufficiently extensive and efficient instrumentality having been as yet established to meet the claims thus arising – while great and growing evils are found to be inseparable from individual and indiscriminate almsgiving – An association be now formed.[1]

These women, thereby, joined thousands of others across the Western world who also established voluntary associations for charitable purposes during the nineteenth century.

This entry from the LBS's minute-book provides a useful guide about where to seek answers about the nature and significance of these women's endeavour. First, members' self-identification as women and the LBS's formation as a single-sex society betray the significance of gender identity and ideology. Second, that the association's founding was initiated by members of local religious denominations, exclusively although not explicitly Protestants, and its aim to provide "Christian beneficence" indicates that religion was centrally important to motivating and justifying this endeavour. These women's access to the local grammar school, their literacy, and the leisure and funds that enabled them to form this association should also attune us to the importance of class in facilitating the LBS's goals. Lastly, the LBS's mandate to establish a "sufficiently extensive and efficient instrumentality" to counteract "indiscriminate almsgiving" signals this association's intention to innovate and modernize charitable provision in Hamilton by introducing the principles and practices of "scientific charity."

Since the LBS ultimately relied on both private (voluntary) and public (state) contributions, these women were obliged to make their association's aims and objectives congruent with that which was understood as the public good. Evangelical Protestantism, middle-class formation, and gender ideologies helped to legitimize the LBS's work and justify its existence. In addition, the LBS's appropriation of techniques of scientific charity, including investigations of applicants for aid, categorizing the deserving and undeserving poor, and eliding recipients' subjective narratives, connected the association to a transnational project of charitable innovation. Scientific charity's borrowings from corporate business models and its emphasis on systematic management, fiscal economy, and administrative transparency also helped make the LBS's endeavours acceptable to those most able to assist the association – namely, property-owning men.

Voluntary associationalism is a complex cultural phenomenon that emerged out of the joint stock revolution of the 1690s. At this time, Western capitalists with relatively small sums of money to invest recognized that if they pooled their resources they could finance projects that required very large investments, such as building canals and bridges.[2] By the late eighteenth century, the joint stock model had been appropriated by would-be philanthropists throughout the Western world. Prior to the mid-eighteenth century, philanthropy had been the exclusive purview of the very rich. Associational charity allowed men and women of the new middle classes to subscribe relatively small sums of money to undertake significant benevolent endeavours, such as building asylums or hospitals. These individuals could also distinguish themselves from less benevolent others whose names did not appear on the subscription lists and membership rolls that circulated locally.

Charitable work played a key role in middle-class formation. Middle-class men reserved for themselves roles in politics, business, and civil society, while their female kin were delegated responsibility for familial, moral, and religious life. Women of the middle classes were largely put in charge of the poor.[3] Charity provided women with opportunities to emulate their male kin's roles in voluntary and joint stock associations, by which they too acquired skills, developed competencies, and asserted authority over others. Middle-class men's appropriation of leadership positions and the prerogative to define the public good made charitable women's work possible. Their female kin, in turn, gave moral substance to the middle class's claims to political and cultural authority.[4]

Evangelical Protestantism was another factor that altered the practice and scope of Western philanthropy. By the late eighteenth century, the notion that both individuals and society could be reformed had begun to gain credence throughout Britain, Northern Europe, and North America.[5] The Calvinist philosophy of pre-destination had been in decline in many American towns and villages since the mid-eighteenth century. Jonathan Edwards's evangelical theology, which proposed that Christ's saving grace was available to all believers who were willing to renounce sin and dedicate their life to God, was especially appealing to new Americans who expected to better their conditions on earth and were therefore less willing to accept that they could not improve their standing in the afterlife as well.

Evangelicalism also challenged the notion of pre-millennialism, which foresaw Christ's second coming after an apocalyptic era of tribulation. Edwards's post-millennial theology forecast that all of society could be reformed on Christian principles, and once a thousand years of Christian peace reigned over the world, Christ would return. This perspective on the millennium motivated evangelicals to put their faith into practice through good works and missionary activity.[6] Carroll Smith-Rosenberg identifies Jacksonian evangelicals' optimism about the perfectibility of mankind and their desire to hasten the millennium as an "impetus and motivation" to New York City missions amongst the poor.[7] By the 1830s, according to Michael Gauvreau, evangelical Protestants in Canada, like Edward and Lydia Jackson, had embraced the idea that "their movement would transform society by a slow permeation of Christian values and conduct" and the millennium could be realized by converts who would "'voluntarily' combine in civic associations for the purposes of social improvement."[8]

Evangelical Protestantism's impetus for charitable organizing also facilitated the entry of women into this field. Women always composed the majority of enthusiastic converts at evangelical revivals and awakenings in the United States and Canada. Women also predominated in the respectable congregations of nineteenth-century evangelical churches. Evangelical preachers encouraged women's involvement in various church activities, including charitable associations. Charity work offered evangelical women an outlet for their talents and energies that abided by both gender and religious expectations.[9]

Hamilton's Ladies' Benevolent Society's active membership was composed entirely of Protestant women.[10] Its executive customarily included the wives of the town's Presbyterian, Anglican, and Methodist ministers, in addition to other prominent women from these congregations. A portion of the Society's funding was also generated by local Protestant churches. Between 1846 and 1850, approximately £134 of its total revenue of £864 was collected directly from the churches. These donors represented a range of theological and dogmatic positions on the Protestant continuum, which included Anglicans, Baptists, Wesleyan and Episcopal Methodists, and both Free Church and United Presbyterians.[11]

Evangelical Protestants figured prominently amongst British reformers who, by the end of the eighteenth century, began to advocate for the application of science to charitable provision. They believed that the scientific method could lead to rational solutions to the problem of poverty.[12] Sir Thomas Bernard, an evangelical who founded the Society for Bettering the Conditions of the Poor in 1796, was a particularly influential advocate for the science of the poor. Bernard called for a "new ordering of knowledge" and argued that the living conditions of the poor must be "investigate[d] practically, and upon system." The Society collated data that was gathered from hundreds of philanthropic experiments and documented their findings with "deductions from facts" in widely publicized annual reports.[13]

Empirical findings were meant to generate solutions that would permanently ameliorate the conditions in which the poor lived and ensure that charitable funds were spent efficiently and only on the most needy and deserving. In England, these innovations were compatible with the utilitarian and laissez-faire economic policies that were largely responsible for the Poor Law Amendment Act of 1834, which sought to dramatically decrease charitable expenditures and thereby tax rates. The notion of less eligibility and the workhouse test were also putatively "rational" responses to widespread poverty.

Political economists and evangelical theologians argued that without a scientific basis, charitable giving only palliated poverty and was thus detrimental to society as a whole.[14] These reformers railed against what they pejoratively referred to as "indiscriminate almsgiving," which was ostensibly unsystematic, inefficient, and perpetuated rather than mitigated dependence.[15] The LBS's appropriation of this epithet reiterates the concern that the poor in Hamilton were becoming more, rather than less, dependent on charity (the "great and growing evils" to which its inaugural statement presumably refers). It also signals the founders' intention to emulate scientific innovations to charitable practice.

The techniques of scientific charity empowered philanthropists to intervene into and regulate the lives of others to an unprecedented degree. Thomas Malthus, for example, argued that charity must be "acquainted with the objects which it relieves ... enters their houses, informs itself not only of their wants, but of their habits and dispositions."[16] The visiting society, which was the charitable model adopted by the LBS, was based on precisely this principle. This model was most famously adopted by evangelical theologian Thomas Chalmers who became particularly renowned for his visiting schemes, which were widely emulated.[17] By the mid-nineteenth century, hundreds of visiting societies had been established in Britain, Europe, and North America.[18]

Normative gender roles that delegated guardianship over the domestic sphere to women helped legitimize their participation in domiciliary visiting societies.[19] These charities empowered middle-class women to take on many of the same tasks for which they were responsible in their own homes: tending to the sick, providing meals and clothes, protecting and caring for young children, and "put[ting] the houses of the poor in order."[20] Although respectable women visiting the poor to dispense food, clothing, or fuel was a very old practice in most parts of the Western world, the introduction of systematic organization to the home visit marked a crucial change in charitable practices internationally between 1780 and 1850.[21]

In the United States and Britain, published versions of visitor instruction manuals, constitutions, and annual reports circulated widely, and the LBS's founders appear to have modeled their association on these international examples.[22] All who wished to become a visiting society member paid a subscription fee, which in the case of the LBS was five shillings. A board of administrative officers – identified as the Committee of Management – was chosen annually from the membership. These included a president, three vice presidents, recording secretary, secretary of accounts, and treasurer, as well as a number of committee members-at-large.[23] The LBS's Committee of Management's duties, as well as detailed rules governing the Society's administration, were itemized and recorded in minute books.[24]

One of the Committee of Management's first duties was to divide the town into sixteen "wards" to which two "Visitors" were assigned. Any member whose dues were paid was eligible to act as a visitor. Ward visitors were assigned "the sole charge and superintendence" of their ward.[25] The LBS printed tickets, which were distributed throughout Hamilton's neighbourhoods to notify residents that, for example, Martha Gale Law was the visitor for Ward 4, and applicants living in that ward ought to direct their claims to her. Tables were also printed and distributed that itemized each visitor's name, residence, and ward. Upon receiving an application, visitors were charged with conducting a "personal investigation" into the case before providing any relief. If she saw fit to do so, a visitor was allowed to provide relief in the form and amount of her choosing. She would, however, have to answer for her decisions at the Society's monthly meeting when she submitted her written report to the treasurer, which had to include the names of persons to whom aid was given, the amount and kind of aid distributed, and an explanation of the applicant's circumstances.

The rationalizing technique of wards, which was borrowed from charitable schemes elsewhere, inscribed in space particular women's authority over others. Authority to superintend, investigate, and reallocate communal funds within these spaces did not empower these women ipso facto, as other historians might suggest. LBS visitors' power was accrued to them by race, class, and gender norms that delegated responsibility for charity to white, middle-class women, as well as a transnational culture of philanthropy that legitimized their rationalized and social scientific methods.

During its first year of operations, the LBS's president, Elizabeth Thomas, regularly instructed visitors to use "circumspection" and "vigilant carefulness" when distributing relief. She directed them to exercise "as much economy as possible" and never accede to requests "without personal inspection."[26] Thomas also reminded visitors that written reports had to be complete and submitted on time "in order that the amounts of the [accounting] secretary be regularly kept."[27] The president adhered to methods that advocates of scientific charity asserted were effective, efficient, and rational. These concerns, on the one hand, were congruent with contemporary notions about charitable best practices and, on the other, would have been crucial to making the association's affairs acceptable to those in positions of formal and informal power.

The annual meeting was another technique borrowed from joint-stock companies and adapted to nineteenth-century associational charities. This event was a particularly important opportunity for the LBS to make its affairs known to the general public. Although most prominent members of this relatively small community would have already been aware of the Society's work, the annual meeting, like its corporate cousin, provided transparency and therefore accountability to supporters and stakeholders.

The LBS's annual meetings were announced in Hamilton's newspapers and from the pulpits of local Protestant churches, and were open to any and all who wished to attend. This annual event was held in City Hall from 1847 until 1854, when the meetings were moved to the Society's boardroom in its own facilities. The president presided as chair and also recited the customary prayer. During the meeting, regular business was attended to and elections for executive and visitors' positions held. A prepared report that detailed the association's affairs, including its financial records, was read out by the secretary and later published in the newspapers and distributed in pamphlet form.

Annual general meetings and annual reports, which became standard practices for associational charities in the nineteenth century, were important mechanisms used by LBS's managers to represent their association to the public. Annual reports are fundamentally rhetorical: their purpose – then as now – was to defend and justify past actions, attempt to create consensus amongst an audience in support of particular objectives, and direct future actions.[28] The LBS's female Committee of Management exercised authorial control over these texts and, in some cases, used particular rhetorical strategies to secure public approbation. Their invocation of categories of deserving and undeserving poor, for example, assured the public that the LBS was a well-regulated institution and supporters could trust that their charitable donations would not be misspent.

These women could, to an extent, use the annual report to influence public opinion. Since the LBS's very existence relied on its managers' capacity to secure favourable public opinion, however, their rhetoric had to be consonant with public opinion as it already existed. In other words, although annual reports' authors could, in theory, introduce rhetoric that was contrary to public opinion, they could not do so and remain viable as a voluntary charitable association. Insofar as public opinion and the public good were negotiated in the realm of the public sphere, women's rhetorical acts were constrained by a discursive field constituted by property-owning men.

The LBS's annual reports adhered to a standard format and changed surprisingly little over time. Customarily, reports expressed the female managers' wish that the report would receive the approbation of "the public" and that the Society would continue to warrant its supporters' "liberality." Next, a few statements about the challenges faced and overcome by the LBS in the past year were introduced. A brief statement outlined the amount and kind of aid distributed. Occasionally, statements about the association's purposes, rules and regulations, and administrative issues were included. Reports almost always made specific arguments about the public good accrued from the LBS's efforts. Its future plans and prospects were mentioned, which were usually followed by an appeal for an increase in public support. Each report concluded with a prayer for God's blessing.

As an example, the Society's first annual report was offered by the Committee of Management "with the hope that it may be approved of, and public confidence in the Society increased."[29] The report noted the "great liberality and kindness" shown by "the public" in the past year and itemized the aid these donations allowed the LBS to distribute. During the year, the committee explained, "many cases of deep distress" were encountered, which the LBS had been able to "alleviate." As well, the Society attended to several cases of "temporary hardship in which a little assistance was of great consequence."[30] The report also made an appeal for additional donations toward a day school, whereby destitute children could be "decently clothed if necessary fed and prepared for future industry and usefulness." In closing, the committee "acknowledge[d] the goodness of Almighty God" for "countenancing" their work.

A significant theme that appears in the first annual report and reoccurs consistently is the effectiveness of the home visit as a technique of scientific charity.[31] The Committee of Management admitted in 1847 that it had been "imposed upon in some instances." Undeserving applicants were unable to evade detection, however, "as the system of visitation steadily pressed soon brought to light the real circumstances."[32] In 1850, the Committee claimed that, "notwithstanding the most watchful diligence and care, the visitors continue to find that in many instances their charity is misplaced." The "regular system of visitation which is pursued by the society," according to the report, "frustrates in a great degree the attempts at imposition that are met with."[33] These reports assured the public that, despite fraudulent claims, the home visit prevented undeserving applicants from receiving charity and, therefore, the LBS could be trusted to manage charitable funds judiciously.

LBS annual reports also claimed that some individuals brought poverty upon themselves, through intemperance, improvidence, vice, or indolence, which rendered them undeserving of the Society's and the public's assistance.[34] In contrast, the sick, the aged, women, and children were deemed generally deserving of charity.[35] Indeed, the LBS's visiting records, which are most descriptive during the years 1846 to 1850, confirm that the Society directed its aid at the "traditional poor": the young, the old (frequently widows), and those with an illness or disability.[36] Between June 1846 and July 1848 the LBS distributed aid to 183 women, 18 men, 6 families, and 8 children. Most of the women had no male provider, were elderly, ill, and/or disabled themselves and/or had children who were ill, dying, or disabled.

Although ward visitors undoubtedly had intimate contact with the recipients of aid, compelled as they were to conduct a "personal investigation" of all applicants' circumstances, very few evocative descriptions of the daily struggles of poor families or the personal calamities that precipitated poverty were included in annual reports. A rare example appeared in the second annual report in which the Committee of Management identified scenes "truly appalling, such as sick persons with nothing but a roof to cover them, frozen to the floor upon which they lay ... and mothers sick and desolate deprived at once of husband and children by pestilence."[37] These images were not common features in the reports, however.

The customary method used in annual reports to explain the visiting society's work was to provide statistical accounts of the amount and kind of aid distributed. The following is a typical description, excerpted from the 1854 report: "181 families have been relieved by the Visitors; they have received 5002 loaves of bread, 161 loads of wood, and groceries to a considerable amount, in a few cases bedding and clothing have also been given."[38] In another example, from 1863, the annual report stated, "190 families have been relieved during the year" to whom the Society provided "3,532 loaves of bread, ... 299 loads of wood, and over 100 articles of wearing apparel."[39] These statements were identified as "facts laid before the Public."[40]

Sandra Sherman argues that nonliterary texts produced in the last decade of the eighteenth century in England "*imagined* the poor by reconstituting their reality through quantifying protocols that submerged individual narrative – subjectivity – in statistics, input/output rations, and institutional accounts that flattened personal distinctions." According to her analysis, the poor "were abstracted, homogenized, put at a distance by an 'avalanche of printed numbers' that replaced human beings in bourgeois readers' minds."[41]

Despite its claims to validity and verifiability, quantification was a process of imagination that helped middle-class readers to "see the poor without unique desires and complex subjectivity." It thus "became plausible, indeed justifiable, to alter old, ethical protocols of relief, which accorded the poor nominal choices and recognized their prerogative, however slight, to bargain face-to-face for what they claimed to need and deserve."[42] When the poor were imagined in statistical terms, the subjective narratives of individual or collective experience were suppressed, which prevented empathetic reactions in the audience.

The LBS's attempt to generate statistical information about the poor in Hamilton, who were referred to generically as "families," was clearly influenced by transnational trends toward a rationalized science of charity. Quantification technologies such as the annual report also facilitated an elision of particular groups' social experiences from the public view. Depersonalization of the poor helped naturalize the relative positions of property owners as active citizens and non-property owners who had no legitimate claim to political participation or citizenship. Despite tacit and explicit claims to objectivity, highly consequential political and social categorizations were embedded in numerical representations of poverty in Hamilton.[43]

The single most important theme that reoccurred most often in annual reports, even more than pleas for financial assistance, was that of God's countenance of the Society's work. In the context of mid-nineteenth-century Canadian Protestant culture, the moral and historical authority of a Christian ontology was irrefutable. This was a culture deeply influenced by the idea that the bible was a true record of past, present, and future that testified to the unfolding of God's design.[44] Divine endorsement was a very powerful claim to convince the public of the rationality and rectitude of the Society's work. The claim that God endorsed the Society's endeavour also obscured its association with Protestant evangelical Christianity specifically, which potentially deflected criticisms of sectarianism and buttressed the Committee of Management's assertions that it served the interests of the Christian community at large.

Nearly every annual report argued that God's blessing was bestowed upon the Society and therefore empowered it to accomplish its mission. The fifth annual report, for example, declared that the committee had "arduous duties to perform – but being assured their cause is good they hope to be able to overcome the difficulties which may arise and leave the result with God."[45] The reports insisted that the Society's successes were evidence of God's approbation. In 1857, the committee expressed "constant trust in Providence which watches over and approves their efforts" and vowed to continue its work "believing by their success that they are not labouring in vain."[46]

Annual reports also argued that God commanded the Society's work and its members were "fellow workers" with Christ. In 1854, for instance, the report declared that the committee "look[ed] forward to another year of active usefulness ... with the blessing of Him who took little children in his arms and blessed them, who went about continually doing good, and who left us an example that we should follow His steps."[47] Rather than invoke maternal metaphors to explain the association's work, which, once the LBS began operating an orphans' asylum in 1848, would have been especially relevant, annual reports argued that the association's work was Christ-like. In 1863, one report asked rhetorically, "Did not our Saviour set us the example of going about doing good? Did he not take young children in his arms and bless them? Is it not then a privilege to become a fellow-worker with Christ?"[48]

The Committee of Management's appeals to a Christian public and assurances of God's approbation demonstrate both an internalization of religious commitment and the extent to which religion, in this case, evangelical Protestantism, empowered these women to accomplish their charitable goals.[49] The committee's discursive appeal to Christianity in its annual reports was certainly not in any way artful. Protestant, evangelical Christianity was integral to these women's understandings of themselves and their place in the world. It also proved to be particularly effective rhetoric with which to justify their authority over the redistribution of private and public charitable funds.

Perhaps the most remarkable thing about these texts is what they did not include. Over the course of the nineteenth century, annual reports did not once claim that the managers were particularly suited to their work because they were women. This is particularly striking because charitable women's work, especially on behalf of orphans and dependent children, could have been so easily likened to mothering roles. LBS managers' avoidance of maternal metaphors or references to women's special capacity for charitable work also is notable considering how prevalent these justifications were in Victorian culture more generally.

Why would this have been the case? Nineteenth-century women's appropriation of rhetorical power was potentially problematic. Karlyn Kohrs Campbell explains that, in nineteenth-century America, "femininity and rhetorical action were seen as mutually exclusive. No 'true woman' could be a public persuader."[50] Rhetorical activity was gendered male; therefore, any woman's rhetorical acts "unsex[ed]" her.[51] Female members of the LBS who exercised authorial control over persuasive writing addressed to the public risked harsh judgment.

The absence of references to women's gender identities may have mitigated these rhetorical offences. According to Nancy Isenberg, women in antebellum America were able to influence public opinion through the written word to an extent that would have been impossible if they had attempted public speech. As long as women remained "authors whose reasoned arguments appeared only in print, they could influence public debate." Women's capacity to participate in a literary public sphere, she argues, "depended on their disembodiment."[52] Annual reports, which were primarily disseminated in print, provided a figurative veil behind which charitable women's gender remained obscure. Their gender-neutral rhetoric would have had a similar effect.

Also, according to the patriarchal ideology upon which the public sphere was based, women's gender particularity undermined their ability to speak on behalf of the public. As Harold Mah explains, the public sphere was not "a space for the free expression of disagreeing social identities and interests." It was a political phantasy that functioned to "fuse persons into a collective, unitary subject, no longer a 'public sphere' but now 'the public.'"[53] Charitable women could not represent themselves as women, who, unlike men, were assumed to embody particular gender interests, whilst presuming to act as carriers of public opinion. To appeal to the public as Christians rather than women was, however, more likely to elicit the response that the Committee of Management sought, which was to convince those most capable of supporting their Society that it served an objective, rational, and universal public good.

As a voluntary charitable society, the LBS's most important task was to establish its legitimacy. Without general public approbation, the association could not secure the donations that made its charitable work possible. The LBS's success depended wholly on general recognition as an acceptable and well-managed association. In part, the association's legitimacy was derived from established religious, racial, class, and gender norms that delegated charitable roles to evangelical Protestant, white, middle-class women. It also relied on a transnational culture of philanthropy to provide models and techniques that would be generally accepted as valid and effective – namely, those of scientific charity.

The LBS's Committee of Management also had at its disposal the annual report, which could be used to make specific arguments about the association's contributions to the public good. To the extent that these arguments were convincing, the LBS could build and consolidate support. These rhetorical acts did not, of course, exist in a vacuum. Although the Committee exercised some degree of control over annual reports, their capacity to represent themselves and their work was also constrained by the limits of public opinion and the patriarchal ideology upon which the public sphere was based. The association's success, evinced in part by the cooperative relationship established with city council discussed in the following chapter, demonstrates that the committee was particularly effective at negotiating the discursive terrain available to them.

3

A Mixed Social Economy

In the years between 1847 and 1850, Hamilton's civic leaders faced unprecedented challenges, due in large part to the mass migration of thousands of Irish Roman Catholics escaping poverty and starvation in their homeland. The city struggled to cope with large numbers of sick, homeless, and destitute immigrants because it lacked any institutionalized social welfare or medical services. In the absence of relevant legislation, Hamiltonians nonetheless seemed to assume that the City Corporation bore at least some responsibility for those who were utterly incapable of taking care of themselves. The City and citizens were therefore compelled to improvise solutions to the social problems they faced. In 1847, the City provided almost no support for communal dependants. By 1850, it had established a public Board of Health (albeit ad hoc) and House of Industry, as well as a public-private partnership that partially funded a permanent orphans' asylum operated by the LBS. The case of the Hamilton Orphan Asylum demonstrates that partnerships between the state and nominally private charitable associations have a longer history than many Canadian historians have heretofore acknowledged.

Mariana Valverde opened this discussion in 1995 when she argued that a "mixed social economy" was a "Canadian tradition." She encouraged historians to reject the binary opposition of public and private in social welfare history and interrogate the political and social implications of this rhetorical construction.[1] Valverde identifies the origins of the public/private dichotomy as liberal political philosophy, namely a laissez-faire economic model that glorified the principle of free enterprise, which "created the illusion that civil society was quite autonomous." This illusion was straightforwardly political in that it "governed differential access to government subsidies" that various residents could expect to have.[2] To whom charitable grants from the state would go depended largely on would-be philanthropists' political capital.[3] Those private associations that most reflected the values and purposes of the state were likeliest to receive support. Despite its significance, few Canadian historians have systematically analyzed the effects of liberal political philosophy on charitable endeavours during the pre-1875 period.[4]

Child charities in fact may have been unique in the degree to which governments were willing to become involved financially and administratively. In his study of nineteenth-century American orphanages, Timothy Hasci notes that, in the case of child welfare, the "line between 'private' charity groups and 'public' welfare bureaucracies" was "fluid."[5] He explains that, during the nineteenth century, both municipal and state governments in the United States often used "private agencies" to provide "a public service" by caring for dependent children. Governments often recognized that asylums provided services more cheaply than they could have done – presumably because they were operated on volunteer labour – and "governments often paid the asylums accordingly."[6]

Although the City was far from eager to assume responsibility for those who could not care for themselves, with the arrival of the famine Irish in large numbers in Hamilton beginning in 1847, its hand was forced. In an attempt to deal with immigrants who arrived with serious illnesses and to prevent diseases from spreading into the community, city council established a board of health. This board set up a hospital for immigrants near Hamilton's waterfront, hired nurses and constables – reputedly for immigrants' protection – and promoted sanitation measures around the city.[7] Although the provincial government agreed to cover the costs incurred by the hospital (at the pleading of Hamilton's mayor), the City struggled to cope with social welfare issues precipitated by the famine migrations.[8] In November, one thousand destitute immigrants, who were without work or adequate shelter to get them through the winter, languished in Hamilton.[9]

According to Brian Clarke, "the Great Famine overwhelmed contemporaries."[10] In terms of institutional and financial resources, this certainly was the case in Hamilton. The city had no hospital or health department as of 1847, and the local jail functioned as its only public welfare institution. Hamilton's municipal government was wholly unprepared to cope with the volume of immigration or the destitute and diseased condition of some of the immigrants when they arrived. Fraternal societies such as St. George's and St. Andrew's had charity committees; extant records suggest, however, that their resources were meagre and more attention was paid to socializing than fundraising.[11] Plus, these associations helped only their own countrymen, which meant that the St. Patrick's Society, for example, would have been easily overwhelmed. The LBS was the only charitable organization of its kind in Hamilton, and it initially refused to assist immigrants.

In June 1846, the LBS established a policy that immigrants, "while in the receipt of aid from government," would not be assisted by the Society.[12] This policy suggests that the LBS assumed that immigrants were the provincial government's responsibility, which was a position evidently shared by the City as well. Since the province provided free grants and subsidized immigrants' passages at various times during the 1840s, both the City and the LBS argued that immigrants had no legitimate claims upon local relief. The City went so far as to complain that relief for immigrants was a "heavy burden ... unjustly imposed" upon it by the province.[13]

In Britain, the poor were traditionally considered to be a local responsibility, hence the very old practice of transporting relief claimants back to the place of their birth or last known residence. Municipalities and voluntary charities tended to insist, therefore, that only locals and long-time residents qualified for their aid. Although this was a convenient way of dodging financial responsibility for peripatetic beggars, the principle had a certain logical orderliness about it, especially when people tended not to move around over long distances. Large-scale, international immigration seriously challenged this logic.

When the LBS was requested in June 1847 to provide clothing for immigrant children "taken from the sheds," the Society did not invoke the argument that immigrants were "strangers" or that they were the provincial government's responsibility. In this case, it justified its refusal on the grounds that any assistance to immigrants "should enduce [sic] many to remain in Hamilton" instead of migrating further west where "work is more easily procured."[14] The LBS argued that ample opportunities could be found on the province's agricultural frontiers and, therefore, immigrants ought not to be encouraged to stay in the city. This instance also demonstrates that the Society was more concerned about rigidly adhering to policies than exercising its humanitarianism. No destitute immigrant parent likely remained in Hamilton simply because their child was decently dressed.

In spite of all evidence to the contrary, newspaper editors, public officials, and the LBS remained convinced that immigrants could be easily integrated into Canada West's economy as agricultural labourers.[15] Few, even hale and hearty men, could find such work, especially once winter descended. Those who were broken by disease and near-starvation, as well as scores of women and children who found themselves widowed, orphaned, and friendless in a strange land, faced exceedingly poor prospects.

Despite the LBS's reluctance to provide aid to immigrants, the migration of thousands of Roman Catholic Irish into the city began to take a toll, directly and indirectly, on the Society's charitable resources. Once immigrants decided to settle in Hamilton and provincial government subsidies were exhausted, destitute newcomers became legitimate claimants upon the LBS's aid. In January 1848, the Society distributed relief in excess of £32, which was nearly double the amount distributed in the same month the previous year.[16] By February, the LBS's funds were "so much reduced," despite recent donations from the churches, that the secretary suggested "some active measures" were needed to get the Society through until the annual ward collections could be taken.[17]

The "measure" devised by the LBS was to petition the City to "take the case of the orphans supported by the Society into their notice and if possible advance funds for the support of an orphan Asylum."[18] This request for financial support from the City was not unprecedented. When the newly incorporated city council met for the first time in January 1847, its agenda included a request from the LBS to pay for "Mrs. Cooper's children" who had been abandoned by their mother and left destitute. The council had acceded to the Society's request.[19]

The LBS committee's decision to propose a formal partnership with Hamilton City Council in 1848 was strategic in that this agreement would establish regular funding for the care of dependent children, over which the LBS would have complete autonomy. The arrangement would also enable the committee to establish a "destitute school" in connection with the asylum, which had been a "desirable object" on its agenda since February 1847.[20] Furthermore, the City's contributions would indirectly subsidize the LBS's outdoor relief for poor mothers, which could forestall the need for custodial care of their children.[21]

The City also had a number of good reasons to cooperate with the LBS. In the United States and Canada during the nineteenth century, in the absence of other options, local governments and officials most often used apprenticeship to cope with children without guardians.[22] Trade apprenticeships had been used in England since the thirteenth century to train boys for skilled occupations, such as tailoring or blacksmithing.[23] Pauper apprenticeship was modeled on this system as a way to provide dependent boys and girls with a home and the training normally provided by a parent.[24]

Hamilton City Council, however, did not have legal rights to apprentice children until its Act of Incorporation was amended in 1849, which empowered the mayor to act as "legal guardian of all orphan or vagrant children within the City" and to "apprentice or bind such children."[25] Even after this point, Hamilton's council, like other similar bodies elsewhere, was often faced with the need to cope with children who were too young or sickly to apprentice or for whom apprenticeships were unavailable. At times, the City needed to protect children whose parent or parents were temporarily unable to care for them, as in the case of illness or imprisonment. The LBS's willingness to take responsibility for these children offered a valuable and economical service to the City Corporation.

In February 1848, Hamilton City Council committed itself to rent and furnish a building, and, for the right to forward children who fell to the public charge, the council paid a fee to the LBS for each child sent into the asylum by the mayor.[26] In return, the LBS agreed to "superintend the establishment and education of the children and find the requisite clothing."[27]

In October 1848, the heavy flow of immigrants compelled city council to re-establish its immigrant hospital. Nonetheless, by February 1849, the Hospital Committee was complaining that the building was too small. At the committee's urging, the City purchased land and began building a hospital, which would also accommodate a workhouse. The Hospital Committee recommended the addition of the workhouse "to prevent in a great measure the street begging which is too common in this City and afford a refuge to the really destitute."[28] After the workhouse began operations in July, the newly formed House of Industry Committee expressed itself "happy to find that applications are not very numerous up to the present." Only five individuals had availed themselves of its services.[29] This strategy reflected post-1834 British social welfare practice, in which the state provided institutional rather than outdoor relief, based at least partially on the belief that only the most desperate would enter into a workhouse. The term *workhouse* was likely a misnomer since residents tended to be incapable of work due to illness, age, or disability. In Hamilton, the House of Industry Committee also struggled to find work to occupy the "inmates."[30]

Nearly five thousand additional Irish immigrants arrived in the town during the 1849 immigration season, which extended from mid-summer to early fall.[31] In May, city council sent another request to the provincial government to help "meet the heavy expenditure" of dealing with a large influx of immigrants.[32] Over a five-month period, the hospital's staff treated 244 immigrants, 66 of whom died.[33] The City had spent approximately £102 on supplies and salaries for the hospital by August, which represented a little more than one-quarter of its total expenditures.[34] In that month, council again requested funds from the province "to stay this deep injury to the revenues of the city."[35] Council also passed two motions indicating that it would not provide aid to immigrants in good health but would assist those who were "evidently destitute or sick."[36]

The migration's volume was at times staggering. Out of the five thousand immigrants who landed on Hamilton's shores in 1849, according to the Emigrant Committee's report, two thousand arrived in the three weeks between August 20 and September 10, 1849. The City supplied bread to "many hundreds" and paid transportation costs for 426 individuals to leave Hamilton. A great many others had apparently been sent off through "private charity."[37] At the time of the report, the immigrant sheds sheltered seven hundred out of the nine hundred immigrants who had arrived the previous Friday and Saturday. Among these, the committee explained, were "many widows with numerous young children and other families quite helpless." The City had, by this point, two charitable institutions on which it could depend. The committee advised that the widows be sent to the House of Industry and their children to the Orphan Asylum.[38]

Hamiltonians were also psychologically unprepared to deal with large numbers of Irish Roman Catholics who remained in the city. These ethnic and religious others flowed into the city after 1847 at a rate that alarmed Hamiltonians. Although a priest had been resident in the town since 1834 and a church was built in 1838, Roman Catholics were a small and inconsequential religious minority. By 1851, Roman Catholics constituted 15.4 percent of Hamilton's population, which made Catholicism the town's largest single denomination. Ninety-four percent of this Catholic population was Irish.[39]

Protestant Hamiltonians often assumed that Irish Roman Catholic immigrants were a degraded lot. In Toronto, Clarke observes, a "continual parade of Irish Catholics at the morning sessions of the police court" led Protestants to conclude that they "were an inassimilable mob, incapable of benefiting from the generous freedoms bestowed by the British crown."[40] In Hamilton, Irish Catholics were singled out by police and convicted out of proportion to their population.

Most arrests were on "moral order charges." These offences, which included vagrancy and drunkenness, as well as being a person of "ill fame," a nuisance, or who wandered around town at night, constituted roughly 50 percent of jail committals in Hamilton between 1843 and 1851. Young Irish women were particularly targeted.[41] Between 1832 and 1851, 60 percent of women arrested were Irish, and three-quarters of these were on drunk and disorderly charges.[42] John Weaver attributes this not to the rise of a criminal class in Hamilton but rather to a fear of Irish immigration and an attendant upsurge in concern about community morals.[43]

Anti-Catholic sentiment generally ran high in Canada West during the 1840s and 1850s. Paula Maurutto identifies several factors that contributed to Protestant antipathy in the province, including the restoration of the Catholic Church in England in the 1840s and a revival of French Catholic nationalism in Canada East.[44] Also, Irish Protestants fanned the flames of sectarian strife with their sometimes aggressive Orangeism that functioned to distinguish them from the Roman Catholic other.[45]

Ultramontanism was also transforming certain features of Catholicism in Canada. Bishop Charbonell's appointment to the diocese of Toronto in 1850 was concurrent with efforts to revitalize Roman Catholicism and assert the Church's primacy in the lives of the laity. Social institutions such as schools, asylums, and charity associations were established, which, in Clarke's words, offered a "cradle-to-grave culture separate from that of the Protestant majority."[46] Evangelical Protestants' aggressive proselytizing made the perceived need for separate Catholic institutions even more acute. In Toronto during the 1850s, "the danger of proselytism by Protestant-controlled social institutions came to alarm Catholics, and many feared that the Irish-Catholic poor were particularly vulnerable to Protestant evangelization."[47] Similar alarm likely motivated Hamilton's Roman Catholics to establish their own charitable visiting society, the St. Mary's Benevolent Society, in 1850.

The LBS's extensive records do not include any evidence to suggest that its visitors proselytized Roman Catholic recipients of their aid. Purchases or distribution of bibles, tracts, or other religious materials are not mentioned; nor were Protestant clergymen enlisted to minister to the sick and poor in the wards. Nonetheless, it is certainly conceivable that ward visitors implicitly or explicitly transmitted critical elements of their own faith in their interactions with the poor, who likely grasped its significance as part and parcel of the aid they did or did not receive.

When the St. Mary's Benevolent Society was founded, the LBS's president, Elizabeth Thomas, met with Mrs. Egan, the president of St. Mary's, apparently to discuss "how far it may be practicable that the catholic work of benevolence and charity may be pursued in common." Thomas reported back to the LBS that the Roman Catholic society had "taken up subscription generally through the town" and that the "objects" of their society were exactly the same as the LBS's. Although Thomas reportedly proposed that the two societies unite in their efforts, St. Mary's Benevolent Society declined the offer.[48]

Thomas also discovered by comparing their lists of recipients that "in almost every instance" individuals were receiving aid from both societies. The LBS, therefore, "unanimously agreed *for the present* to suspend all relief" to Roman Catholics.[49] This decision was in keeping with the LBS's mandate to avoid "imposition" – that is, unwittingly accede to fraudulent requests – and rationalize charitable provision in the city. According to the LBS's records, however, ward visitors continued to give aid to Roman Catholics, "being convinced that they receive no assistance from any other society."[50] In November, the Society revised their policy and agreed that "any Roman Catholic bringing a certificate from the priest to show that they were receiving no aid from the Roman Catholic society, should be relieved by the Visitors according to their wants."[51]

The LBS experienced a considerable decline in demand for their services once the St. Mary's Benevolent Society was established. In the three months prior to the Catholic society's founding, the LBS distributed aid to 136 families; while, in the space of six months after St. Mary's began its work, the LBS assisted only 96 families.[52] Since a Roman Catholic day school had also been set up, there was a sharp decrease in school attendance as well. Although one hundred students attended the LBS's school regularly in March 1850, only seventy students were enrolled in April.[53]

At its annual meeting of 1850, which was held in City Hall, the Society reported that it had a "great decrease" in demand for its services due to the formation of the Roman Catholic Society, since "nine-tenths of those receiving aid [from the LBS] were Roman Catholics." The committee defended its nonsectarianism and assured the public that "in no case" did the LBS ever ascertain an applicant's religion before they were given relief. Furthermore, the Society claimed that it was "generally known" to have been established to provide relief to "all distressed, without reference to creed or country."[54] The LBS reported that, nonetheless, it would not henceforth assist Roman Catholics "unless invited to do so by, and in co-operation with" the St. Mary's Society.[55]

Ultimately, the LBS's charitable work was neither disinterested nor simply humanitarian, its claims to nonsectarianism notwithstanding. Even if it did not proselytize Roman Catholic recipients of aid, the Society's conceptualization of its service for the public good was, of course, political. Ethnoreligious difference compounded the social and economic distance between those who provided and received aid, thereby reflecting, legitimating, and perpetuating local inequalities. Furthermore, as the previous chapter argued, the LBS's charitable method was rooted in a social scientific paradigm that facilitated particular evangelical Protestant, middle-class men's and women's appropriation of leadership roles in their communities.

The City's relationship with the LBS in the care of dependent children was an implicit endorsement of the Society, as well as its particular understanding of the public good. The creation of a charitable association and school by Roman Catholics in Hamilton challenged this understanding. A more critical contestation that was waged by Irish Roman Catholics against the City's collaboration with the LBS in the care of dependent children is the topic of the next chapter.

4
The City and the Ladies

THE COOPERATIVE RELATIONSHIP established in 1848 between Hamilton City Council and the LBS regarding the custodial care and education of Hamilton's orphans came under severe stress when the Society began to agitate for a more significant financial commitment on the part of council. In particular, Roman Catholic councilmen objected to a grant for the asylum on charges of religious proselytism. They argued that the LBS took Roman Catholic orphans and trained them to be Protestants and, therefore, despite the Society's claims, did not deserve public support. Their objection was based on the assumption that city council was bound not to privilege the interests of one religious sect over another. In 1852, with the legal separation of church and state enacted formally one year earlier, the liberal principle of freedom of religion was paid considerable lip service. In the context of local communities such as Hamilton, however, the actual guarantee of that freedom was dependent upon public men's abilities to represent their views as rational and commonsensical in the debates that constituted the public sphere.

Despite the relative stability of the public sphere's political parameters, the particular cohort of men who could claim legitimate access to the public sphere and represent themselves as "the public" was subject to continual contestation. Although the composition of Hamilton's elite during the 1830s and 1840s had changed little, by mid-century immigration had effected significant demographic transformations. The population had more than quadrupled from 3,400 to nearly 14,000 between 1841 and 1852.[1] Although Irish Roman Catholic immigrants were subject to discrimination and relegated to low-status positions generally speaking, by mid-century a handful of Roman Catholics had earned a place amongst the wealthiest men in the city and many more held enough property to vote in civic elections.[2] These Roman Catholic men, who achieved the status of citizen, posed a potential threat to Protestant men's monopoly over formal and informal political power.

The LBS's 1850 annual report declared that the roughcast house rented by the City was "wholly insufficient for securing the health and comfort of the children" and required a large amount of fuel to heat.[3] The Society subsequently approached council with a petition for a grant of city land upon which to establish a permanent site for its asylum.[4] Although council declared that it was willing, in principle, to provide the LBS with a portion of land if it was available, a motion to do so in October 1850 was voted down.[5] This decision was the first indication that council was divided on the issue of whether to establish a more permanent basis for its association with the LBS.

In addition, the Society had placed the council in an awkward legal position. Even if the council was inclined to cede civic space to the Society, the LBS's Committee of Management was composed solely of married women who did not have the legal right to own and manage property.[6] There was, in effect, no one to whom the City could transfer the land. This attempt to procure a building site illustrates one of the barriers faced by women's charitable associations due to their lack of legal and political rights.

The LBS's Committee of Management, however, was able to rely on their personal and social contacts instead to move their project forward. In the face of council's apparent unwillingness to assist the Society, the president, Elizabeth Thomas, appealed directly to the mayor, John Fisher, who was an LBS founder's husband. In a private meeting in December 1850, Fisher explained to Thomas that he could not secure a site for the Society through city council. Nonetheless, he encouraged her to pursue the LBS's plan without the council's assistance.[7] He also made a personal donation of £100 toward the LBS's building fund.[8] Fisher's encouragement and donation spurred the Society into action.[9] The LBS canvassed for donations, petitioned the governor general for a grant, and, by March 1851, raised over £634 toward their building project.[10]

The LBS also appointed a male building committee, which was instructed to select a site for the asylum, apply to the provincial legislature for a charter of incorporation, and fulfill "all such other duties as may be expedient for perfecting" the institution.[11] This decision to transfer some of the project's financial and legal responsibilities to a male advisory committee enlisted the assistance of sympathetic allies endowed with skills, contacts, and legal rights not otherwise at the disposal of the Society. The LBS chose businessmen and civic officials who were married to Society members and had access to power and influence within the political public sphere.

Timothy Hasci notes that while most orphan asylums in nineteenth-century America were managed by women who oversaw the daily operations of their institution, "almost all orphan asylums had male boards of advisers."[12] As a Canadian example, Janice Harvey also found that the Protestant Orphan Asylum and Ladies' Benevolent Society in Montreal established men's committees "when the task at hand fell clearly within the male sphere and/or required specialized knowledge and business contacts."[13]

The Building Committee was composed of John Fisher, Edward Jackson, E. Cartwright Thomas, and John Young, who purchased a site on Wellington Street in October 1851, drafted a charter of incorporation, and petitioned city council for a grant of money for the building project on the LBS's behalf.[14] The Building Committee's request elicited a response from council, which appointed a special committee, composed of Thomas N. Best, James Williams, William Distin, Dennis Moore, Jasper Gilkison, J.B. Dayfoot, and Edward Jackson, to look into the matter.[15]

The city council's committee could not be accused of impartiality. Dennis Moore's wife, Anne, was an LBS visitor, and Edward Jackson, whose wife, Lydia, was the Society's treasurer, was a member of its Building Committee. Nor was the committee a representative cross-section of religious perspectives on council. Despite a contingent of Roman Catholics in City Hall, all members of the Special Committee were Protestants.[16]

Perhaps unsurprisingly, the council committee's report urged the City to support the LBS's "laudable undertaking." Committee members justified their recommendation by reminding council that it already paid the asylum's rent and for services provided by the LBS. This included a school for destitute children and substantial relief to the "outdoor poor," which were "a great saving to our City funds." Furthermore, they explained, the "disinterested exertions of the Ladies" provided relief and education to "every child of misfortune without reference to Creed or Colour." The committee thus recommended a grant of £300 toward the asylum project.[17]

Not everyone on council agreed with this assessment; nor did they accept the committee's recommendation. In particular, Councillor C.J. Tracy, an Irish Roman Catholic proprietor of a boot and shoe store and representative for St. Patrick's Ward,[18] objected to the grant and accused the LBS of proselytizing Roman Catholic orphans.[19] Tracy moved to establish a new committee to "enquire into the Rules and Regulations of the Orphan Asylum," which was passed, but only by a tie-breaking vote cast by the Anglican mayor, John Holden.[20]

The second Special Committee, composed of Tracy, Charles Gray, Joseph Clement, Thomas Best, and Dennis Moore, subsequently arranged to visit the orphan asylum and assess the situation.[21] This committee included two members of the first Special Committee, Thomas Best and Dennis Moore, and, notably, excluded Edward Jackson, who was most obviously partial to the LBS's request. Only one of three new committee members, C.J. Tracy, is known to have been a Roman Catholic.

In response to Tracy's written request for permission to visit the institution, Elizabeth Thomas informed him that "the Orphan Asylum is at all times open to the inspection of its numerous supporters" and that the Committee of Management would meet council's representatives willingly. The subsequent interview, according to the LBS records, "partook rather of a rigid cross examination of the committee and matron, relative to alleged interference with the privileges of Roman Catholics, than of a general enquiry into the nature and regulations of the Institution." The women who met with the council's committee were, however, confident that their "thorough and complete refutation of the charges ... must have convinced such persons as sought only to elicit *truth* that there never has been grounds for the ascertions [sic] that the friends of the asylum had endeavoured to proselytise Roman Catholics, or had otherwise interfered with the just rights and privileges of that or any other sect."[22]

Despite the women's confidence, the second Special Committee's report to council criticized the LBS severely. First, the report condemned the LBS's administrative abilities. The committee argued it was impossible to submit a full report of the asylum's management since there were "no printed or written Rules submitted to their Inspection." In the committee's opinion, the absence of written rules "clearly shewed [sic] that the Orphans are subject to whatever rules the Matron may dictate" and left an impression "not at all favourable to the manner in which the Asylum has been conducted." This criticism illustrates the importance, and perhaps failure, of the LBS's attempts to rationalize its institutional practices and convince the public that its institution was well-regulated. Despite their efforts, council's committee found grounds on which to disparage the Society's management.

The second Special Committee also reported that the LBS members engaged in "some disultory [sic] conversation, and the reading [of] a Report which had nothing to do whatever with the matter under investigation." This report argued that LBS members demonstrated – by their lack of rules, desultory conversation, and meaningless reports – that the Orphan Asylum was poorly managed and that the LBS's executive lacked the necessary skills to properly administer a publicly funded institution. In other words, the committee denied that the LBS had any legitimate claim upon public approbation or public funds.

According to its report, the committee "respectfully suggested to the Office-Bearers the propriety of having the Mayor or some other member of the Corporation to be *ex officio* members of the Board of Management of the Institution." The LBS's executive insisted that "no such interference could be permitted."[23] The committee seemed to suggest that it would be more favourably disposed to the LBS's request for a grant if the Society agreed to defer some of its authority to the council, which the LBS was apparently unwilling to do.

Secondly, the Special Committee accused the LBS of religious proselytism. On the basis of its inspection, the committee reported that "the Orphans are not asked their religious belief, when admitted," "prayers, written on sheets of paper, apparently for examination, are used therein," and "the children are taken by the Matron to attend Divine Service in the English Church, on every Sunday." This proved to the committee that the asylum "cannot give general satisfaction, inasmuch as 'nine-tenths' of the Orphans in the City, could not comply with them without first sacrificing their religious belief."[24]

The report argued that Roman Catholic children brought to the asylum could not worship in their parent's religion; nor were they trained according to Roman Catholic principles. Quite the opposite – all children, regardless of their former religious affiliations, were catechized with prayers in the asylum and taken to the Anglican Church. Reasonably, Roman Catholic committee members objected to council's appropriation of tax monies to finance an institution that made Protestants out of Roman Catholic children. The second Special Committee argued that unless the orphan asylum could "give general satisfaction" – that is, serve all residents on an equitable basis – the institution ought not to be supported with public funds.

Although the committee's report was eventually voted down in council,[25] its message was disseminated widely within the community by the local press.[26] The controversy in City Hall subsequently erupted into a full-fledged public debate. By the time of the next meeting, the city council had received several petitions in support of and objecting to the grant. The LBS's male advisors were particularly anxious to counter the second Special Committee's report, which they did in their own petition to council.[27]

Of first importance to the LBS's Building Committee was to call attention to the aspersions cast by the Special Committee on the asylum's managers. In particular, the Building Committee took umbrage at the suggestion that the testimony of LBS managers, "unsupported by such written or printed rules," was deemed "unworthy of credence." The male defenders of the LBS neglected to offer evidence or testimony that the management and operation of the asylum was, indeed, subject to numerous explicit and written rules.[28] Instead, the Building Committee's ire was raised on the implicit suggestion that the female managers were untrustworthy or dishonest.

The Society's male advisors also objected to the manner in which the women had been treated. The Building Committee claimed that the second Special Committee's investigation had taken the form of a "rigid" and "painful examination" and the members had sought information "in a manner wholly inconsistent with the respect due to the sex and character of the Office-Bearers."[29] The Building Committee deflected attention away from the serious charge of religious proselytism (against which it had few legitimate counter-arguments) by impugning the council's apparently disrespectful and impertinent behaviour toward the LBS's female executive. In other words, the Building Committee attempted to invalidate the council committee's judgment of the LBS by attacking the members' manliness, which demanded chivalrous behaviour toward respectable women.

The LBS's male defenders also implicitly argued that the Society's managers' "sex and character," which called attention to their gender and class status, rendered them above reproach. To put it another way, the Building Committee argued that the LBS ought not to be subjected to the kind of searching investigation that, in the case of similar institutions managed by men, might be justified. The Building Committee nonetheless defended the legitimacy of the LBS's claim upon "the public." The LBS's defenders explained that since "the Asylum courts public investigation, and that it ever has been ready to afford the most ample information to all who may seek such information in a spirit of courtesy," the institution was "entitled to public protection and sympathy."[30] The council committee's investigation was clearly not made "in a spirit of courtesy" and, therefore, apparently lacked merit.

The Building Committee offered additional testimony from "personal knowledge" and "many months of personal acquaintance with the management of the Asylum" that contradicted the second Special Committee's claim that "the Orphans are subject to whatever rules the Matron may dictate."[31] Despite these claims to "personal knowledge" of the management of the asylum, the relationship between the women of the LBS and the Building Committee remained obscure throughout these debates. The Building Committee members' ability to represent themselves as public men rather than husbands protected them from the charges of partiality and interest that would have undermined their defence.[32]

The Building Committee finally addressed the issue of religious proselytism at the end of their report. They explained that children were not asked their religion upon entering the asylum because it was "impossible to ascertain" an accurate statement from very young children. To this they added, "for the most part, the parents and friends of such applicants have been of such abandoned character" that religious classification was "impossible." The Building Committee argued that no asylum "could be properly conducted wherein the inculcation of religious tenets was omitted" and "it follows as a matter of course, that it would be impossible to educate a portion of the Orphans as Roman Catholics, and another portion as Protestants." The committee offered "but one remedy for this difficulty": "Roman Catholics should render Protestant assistance unnecessary, by preserving the offspring of persons of that faith from the state of degradation, disease, and wretchedness, in which such children are constantly found." Until that happened, the asylum's managers, "in the true spirit of that religion which has Christ for its founder," would "continue to succour the destitute, and to provide for the indigent orphan."[33]

Again, the LBS's male defenders invoked women's special status. These women's tasks, to succour the poor and provide for children, were represented as spontaneous and disinterested responses to an apparent need. They also suggested that the LBS's managers acted simply as Christians and, therefore, served the entire community, Protestant and Catholic alike. The Building Committee did not provide any explicit denial that orphans from Roman Catholic families could not be assured protection of and encouragement in their faith within the asylum. They simply suggested that to be reared by Protestants would raise Roman Catholic children out of the degradation into which they would otherwise fall.

Predictably, the Building Committee's arguments ignited Roman Catholic objections to the grant. In response, 530 Roman Catholic "Ratepayers and Citizens" petitioned council and opposed an appropriation of any portion of their taxes to serve "purposes of purely Sectarian character." They did not disapprove of a "grant or appropriation of charitable purposes *generally*" but they were not willing to support any grant "for Protestant purposes *alone*." These petitioners demanded that if a grant was given to the LBS, then "a still larger grant to the St. Mary's Benevolent Society" should be made.[34]

The petitioners also expressed their anger at "the unfounded and unjust reflections – upon Catholics generally" made in the Building Committee's report. They stated, "there is no language they could command or would trust themselves to make use of, sufficiently strong to express their sense of indignation at the gratuitous insults offered." The petitioners could only hope

> that no inscrutable dispensation of an all-wise and all-merciful Providence will ever place John Fisher, John Young, Edward Jackson, and the Sheriff of the United Counties of Wentworth, Halton, and Brant, in such a position (the result of poverty and oppression) as that they or their offspring can, with impunity, be taunted with being "constantly found" in a state of "degradation, disease, and wretchedness."[35]

This impassioned response articulated Roman Catholics' indignation and frustration at their unequal access to power in their community. These petitioners, whose status as ratepayers and citizens qualified them as legitimate discussants in the public sphere, attempted to challenge Protestants' dominance over formal and informal structures of power. The Building Committee could nonetheless disparage Roman Catholics with "impunity" because of their established wealth and status in the community. In particular, Protestant public men wielded the discursive power to redefine the terms of public debate and refashion their interests as common sense.

Other LBS supporters also argued that charitable women were incapable of prejudice and, thus, could not offend Catholic consciences. A petition from "the greater part of the rate-payers of the City," for example, argued that they had full confidence in the managers of the asylum because "these persons have not been selected from the ambitious or the selfish of our community; they are our mothers, our wives, our sisters, our daughters; they love the work in which they are engaged, because it is akin to their own nature."[36] The petitioners argued that these women's work was a manifestation of their "natural" roles as selfless mothers and generous sisters. They were, therefore, unaffected by the public world of competition, selfishness, and prejudice. This rhetoric of female benevolence obscured the authority that the LBS exercised over charitable practice in the city and provided Protestant men with the means to divert attention away from charges of religious proselytism.

Both the LBS's supporters and critics invoked arguments that represented women's charitable work "private" but on different grounds and for different purposes. For Roman Catholic critics, who attempted to protect their religious prerogatives by discrediting the asylum, inefficient management and sectarianism meant that the institution was undeserving of public support and, hence, a private enterprise. According to the LBS's advocates, the "respect due" to female managers ought to protect them from the scrutiny that a public institution would otherwise receive. Women's innate humanitarianism and true Christian spirit also rendered their work politically benign and therefore private. With these rhetorical tactics, Protestant men protected their own interests in and control over the institution.

The LBS's supporters also argued that the Society was engaged in work for which the City would have otherwise been responsible. The Society's economic contribution to the city's welfare was introduced in the first Special Committee's report and in the petition by the "greater part of the rate-payers of the city." The ratepayer's petition, for example, praised the asylum because it was "economical" and "diminished materially the expenditure of the City revenue, which would otherwise have been required under a much more expensive system toward the same object."[37]

A similar argument was offered by Robert Smiley, editor of the *Hamilton Spectator*. Smiley engaged the editor of the Roman Catholic newspaper, the *Canadian*, in a debate over the asylum grant, which was published in their respective papers.[38] The *Canadian*'s editor argued that public money should not be granted in favour of one religious group over another and, if the City was disposed to do so, Roman Catholics deserved a grant more than any other because they represented the largest single religious community in the city. Smiley, who was also a prominent member of the Orange Order, refused to admit that the asylum did harm to Catholic consciences.[39] The question, in Smiley's mind, was "one of £ s. d. [rather] than of sectarianism." He argued, "destitute children of emigrants, or others, whether abandoned by their parents, or left without support by the death of their natural protectors, were of necessity consigned to the funds of the City." Since city council had agreed to share this responsibility with the LBS, "there ought to be no sectarianism in the question, and there need not be any."[40]

Smiley argued that the LBS's request was no different than one to erect a Mechanics' Institute. He asserted that if such a proposal was submitted to the City "on the ground that it was a local undertaking, calculated to advance the interests and prosperity of the citizens at large," parties might object because they "disapproved of the advance of knowledge," but "there would be no one mad enough to designate the variance which might arise between the parties at issue as a 'sectarian struggle.'" The LBS's application was justified because of "the general usefulness of the undertaking, and upon the additional fact of its effecting a saving of the city funds." Smiley insisted that "the Catholic as well as the Protestant are taxed to support the destitute poor, and the Orphan Asylum will provide cheaply and efficiently for a portion of those poor, if the city will remunerate it for doing so."[41]

Smiley deflected the *Canadian*'s editor's complaints with the argument that the asylum provided a necessary service, which accrued benefits to the public at large by saving the City and its taxpayers money. Smiley and other LBS supporters claimed that women's voluntary labour added value to public and private charitable contributions, provided a service that would otherwise require public expenditures and tax increases, and thereby facilitated the capital accumulation of property owners. Although these arguments belied the privacy of women's charitable work, such statements also provided powerful language with which to frustrate Roman Catholic objections. These arguments cast Roman Catholic men as irrational to the point of "madness" and the City's support of the LBS as simply a question of "dollars and cents." In the context of an evolving liberal public sphere, the rationality of fiscal economy was a particularly effective rhetorical device with which to defend the LBS's prerogatives.

Council, meanwhile, was caught in the crossfire of petitions, which ultimately divided its members into competing camps. The only course that was acceptable enough to get a positive vote was to appoint another committee composed of a new combination of councillors to investigate the Society again.[42] On March 20, 1852, a third delegation from the council met with the LBS and its Building Committee.[43] This committee included

Jasper Gilkison, C.J. Tracy, Charles Gray, Joseph Clement, Thomas Best, and Dennis Moore, each of whom had served on one or both of the previous council committees. Aldermen Hatt and Stewart, whose religious affiliations are unknown, were new additions to the group.

The third Special Committee's report, submitted on March 31, concluded that "the Ladies' Benevolent Society, including the Orphan Asylum, are worthy and deserving of the continued countenance and encouragement of the Corporation of this City." The LBS's managers had "afforded ... all possible opportunity of making a searching investigation, even to allowing your Committee to take with them the books of their Society," which, incidentally, included the asylum's rules. On the basis of its investigation into the management, finances, and organization of the LBS and its orphan asylum, the committee declared the institution "to be (considering the limited means) in a most satisfactory and gratifying state." The committee recommended "that in the absence of any publicly endowed charitable Societies, it is proper and just that your Council should not regard with indifference, but lend a helping hand to the disinterested and philanthropic exertions of the more tender sex, who so nobly rescue your city from very many of the evils which flow from pauperism."[44]

This report, like other defences of the LBS, called attention to the Society's status as a female association to explain and justify its work. Council was obliged to countenance and encourage the "more tender sex" because, according to the report, their exertions were "disinterested." The public sphere, as a political discourse, was premised on the notion that only public men's private interests (namely, protection of private property) converged with the common interest, and, thereby, were those who could effectively represent "the public."[45] In this context, female disinterestedness emphasized their privacy. Without an interest that was, by definition, derived from property ownership, women's philanthropy was de facto apolitical. The committee's report also identified charitable women's noble efforts to "rescue" the city from "evil," which portrays the LBS's managers as engaged not in proselytism but Christian heroics.

By casting the council as "a helping hand" that made the LBS's work possible, the committee communicated its intention to extend male authority over the orphan asylum. The committee recommended a grant of £300 "subject to the condition, that His Honor the Mayor for the time shall be a member of the building Committee, and to be named as a Visitor of the Asylum in the proposed Act of Incorporation." This condition addressed one of the second Special Committee's main criticisms, which was that the managers refused to relinquish any of their administrative autonomy.

This report also responded directly to Roman Catholic protests and petitions against the use of their taxes to support a "purely Sectarian" institution. This committee, like others had done before, defended the grant on economic grounds. If the LBS and its asylum "did not exist, a large amount would have otherwise to be paid out of said taxes, to relieve the destitute, and in the punishment of crime."[46] In other words, the LBS served the public good and therefore deserved the City's financial support. The committee's suggestion that the Society mitigated criminal activity added another dimension to the claim of financial savings.[47]

In the course of council's deliberations, the St. Mary's Benevolent Society had requested a share in any grant given to the LBS. The third Special Committee's report also recommended that a grant ought to be given to the Roman Catholic association, to whatever amount "upon investigation [the Society] may appear entitled to." The City did not, however, dispense any money directly to a Roman Catholic association for charitable purposes until 1862.[48] The committee also encouraged the two Societies "to seriously consider and endeavour to unite as one Society, know no distinction, but walk hand in hand in the holy cause of Benevolence and Charity."[49] Acting in his role as member of the council, Edward Jackson said that he "wished to see the two Institutions harmonize," which he believed would so do "if it was not for designing ... wicked men." In the end, this committee's report was passed successfully – by a narrow margin of ten to nine.[50]

When Elizabeth Thomas received council's offer she called a "special general meeting of all the members of the [Ladies' Benevolent] Society" to deliberate on the question of the grant. On March 29, which was after the meeting with the third Special Committee and before its report was read in council, the Building Committee recommended to the LBS that "unless a grant of the City Council be rendered to the asylum by a decided majority of the votes and influence of its members, and be accompanied by an entire and complete refutation of the slanderous charges brought against the Institution," the grant should be "respectfully declined." The LBS had unanimously adopted this recommendation.[51] At this later date, April 5, the report of the third Special Committee and the Building Committee's recommendation were read. On the basis of this information and a subsequent discussion, the LBS's Committee of Management drafted its own resolution.[52]

Harriet Juson, the LBS's secretary, sent a written response to the mayor, which was read out in council and published in the *Spectator.* Juson, on the Society's behalf, expressed "much satisfaction" with the third Special Committee's report. According to her letter, the LBS believed that the report "wholly refuted the unwarrantable charges of proselytizing, and of harshness, and injustice towards Roman Catholics." The executive was also gratified by the "almost unanimous expression of approbation of the management and objects of the Society and of the Orphan Asylum."[53]

Juson's response nonetheless placed considerable importance on the fact that only a "bare majority" voted in favour of the grant despite "the promise of such aid on the part of the Council," which was "of long standing" and "proffered to the Society by the Council on the ground of the usefulness of the Society." Furthermore, she argued, the asylum's objectives "require no eulogy: the advantages of such institutions have been recognized in all civilised countries, and not the less so in this city."[54] Although Juson expressed "much anxiety" and "the deep responsibility of relinquishing an assistance so necessary to its purpose," the LBS could not "fail to be impressed with the undesirableness of acquiring such funds, under the protest of an important minority of the Council, supported by the public opinion of many of the citizens of Hamilton, by whatever sinister designs such opposition may have been obtained." The LBS decided, therefore, "to decline the grant ... and to appeal to public support" with "full confidence that a Christian community will not permit the good work to be frustrated by the perverse and unwarrantable attacks of its opponents."[55]

In contrast to their male defenders, the LBS's response did not refer to gender ideology to support their claims. It explained the Society's deservedness solely on the grounds that city council had agreed to cooperate in the care of dependent children, which saved the City Corporation money. Furthermore, the asylum needed "no eulogy" – all civilized, Christian nations recognized the necessity of such work. Although men such as Edward Jackson asserted that the LBS and St. Mary's Benevolent Society could act in concert, if not for wicked and designing men, Juson's letter explained that an "inability on the part of the Society to co-operate with those whose anti-Protestant principles may prevent an uniformity of design or purpose" was the reason the two groups could not join.[56] Despite men's rhetoric to the contrary, Protestant and Roman Catholic women were clearly not exempt from prejudicial feelings.

The LBS argued that it served the public good and was subject to the rational judgment of informed citizens – even if the judgment of those citizens had been poisoned by "sinister designs" and "perverse and unwarrantable attacks." Without the full approbation of the public the LBS could not make a legitimate claim upon the City's funds, and the protest of an "important minority" justified its decision to decline the council's offer. The LBS simultaneously resisted the City's attempt to renegotiate the terms of its relationship and flatly refused to relinquish their autonomy. The conditions of the grant were simply unacceptable to the LBS managers, who had clearly stated that they would tolerate "no such interference."

This episode demonstrates that Protestant men both within and outside of city council wielded considerable power to define and delimit legitimate participation in the public sphere. By diverting attention away from charges of proselytism, particular men resisted Roman Catholics' attempts to contribute to rational public debate and represent themselves as carriers of public opinion. Protestant men also successfully constructed female charitable work as private, which reaffirmed women's exclusion from the public sphere and, simultaneously, protected the institutionalization of Protestant religious interests in the form of the orphan asylum.

The LBS was a private association and yet the Society's partnership with the City, for which it received a substantial amount of public funding, made the LBS responsible to city council and the constituents it claimed to represent. Although the LBS's managers exercised autonomy over financial and administrative decisions within the orphan asylum, the Society was commissioned by the civic government to act as its agent and charged implicitly with a responsibility to serve the public good. The work of the LBS was clearly implicated in negotiations that constituted a political public sphere in Hamilton.

City council's attempt to exert more control over the LBS's administration was unsuccessful in part because its female managers were confident in their ability to achieve sufficient public support. This confidence derived largely from their male defenders' ability to effectively argue that the LBS's work did indeed serve the public good. General acknowledgment or approbation of the LBS's economic and social contributions did not, however, alter these women's status vis-à-vis the public sphere. Women's exclusion from the public sphere, which was reinforced by rhetorical constructions of women's special status, meant that public men could exercise their power to represent female charitable work in ways that served their own interests.

Once the building grant controversy was over, the LBS still faced the difficult problem of raising sufficient funds for its building project. In April 1852, the Society received a notice from the governor general's secretary that the sum of £125 would be forwarded out of the immigrant fund.[57] With the funds already in hand and several additional donations from supporters, the Society had enough money by the end of August to begin building a new asylum. By this time, the LBS no longer held a monopoly over the care of dependent children in the city. On April 19, 1852, four sisters of St. Joseph arrived in Hamilton at the request of the local priest, Edward Gordon, to establish a Roman Catholic orphans' asylum in the city.[58]

Despite the building grant controversy, the relationship between the LBS and the City was far from over. In the years to come, the Society continued to receive regular payments from city council for orphans sent into the asylum by the mayor. In addition, the provincial government began forwarding an annual grant in 1854. During the period from 1861 to 1871, these two sources of income contributed on average 38.7 percent of the association's total operating budget.[59] Local and provincial government funding meant that the LBS continued to receive the means and the mandate to serve the public good. The terms of that service would be defined formally in an Act of Incorporation approved by the provincial legislature in November 1852.

5
Public Acts and Private Lives

IN MAY OF 1852, in the aftermath of the building grant controversy, the LBS's executive asked its Building Committee, composed of John Fisher, Edward Jackson, E. Cartwright Thomas, and John Young, to frame a document "which in their opinion will be most likely to guard the Institution from trouble or dissension of any kind" and submit it to the legislature for approval.[1] The result of this request was the LBS's incorporation as the Hamilton Orphan Asylum and Ladies' Benevolent Society [HOA/LBS] by an act of the provincial legislature on November 10, 1852.

During the 1840s, the legislative assembly had been inundated with such requests, which resulted, significantly, in 1852, in both a bill endorsing incorporation of charities and a subsequent debate in the assembly.[2] The appropriateness of the state's endorsement of sectarian charity associations was called into question. It was decided, however, that requests for support could not be denied because religious groups were, according to the logic of liberalism, simply associations of free individuals. Incorporation was merely a way "to ensure that the faithful may have optimum conditions in which to exercise their religion freely."[3] This logic conveniently evaded the fact that incorporation empowered sectarian associations to exercise control over charitable recipients' freedom of religion, as in the case of children admitted into the Hamilton Orphan Asylum.

When the Act of Incorporation was passed in November, it designated John Fisher, Edward Jackson, John Young, E.C. Thomas, M. Aikman, J.B. Dayfoot, and Sir Allan MacNab as the association's trustees. The act created a "body politic" that could hold property, sue and be sued, prosecute and be prosecuted, as well as appoint successors. In other words, incorporation transformed the Building Committee, which had been appointed by the LBS, as well as three additional members, into one legal individual with independent, executive authority over both the visiting society's and orphan asylum's administration and assets. Invested with the power to appoint successors and instate or overrule any bylaws, rules, or regulations established by the Ladies' Committee of Management, the trustees effectively usurped these women's control over this institution.

The legitimizing technique of incorporation, executed by public men, integrated the new HOA/LBS into systems of law and governance. Since the act was intended to protect the Society from "trouble or dissension of any kind," male authority over women's charitable work was clearly perceived to have been a necessary and not simply incidental feature of liberal governance. Despite the LBS's successful attempt to avoid interference from Hamilton City Council, incorporation ensured that the new HOA/LBS executive was subject to patriarchal and state authority.

Several historians have observed that in mid-nineteenth-century North America charitable women's groups often lost administrative power to male authorities. Mary P. Ryan argues that by the mid-nineteenth century, American women's associations' management and administration were usually ceded to men.[4] Suzanne Lebsock also found that in Petersburg, Virginia, during the 1850s, single-sex societies were usurped by the rise of mixed associations in which women usually assumed auxiliary roles.[5] In Montreal, Jan Noel identified a similar process whereby women's social welfare work was "overshadowed" by men's initiatives after 1840.[6]

Certainly, the act resolved a legal problem; married women on the Committee of Management, according to *feme covert*, could not hold property or other assets. Nonetheless, the trustees, rather than the institution or the committee, were incorporated, which prevented HOA/LBS women from holding assets on behalf of the corporation. Lebsock, for example, found that the corporate charter of the Orphan Girls Asylum in Petersburg, Virginia, established in 1811, allowed female managers to hold property as a corporation and thus opened "a large loophole in the common-law doctrine of civil death for married women."[7]

Interestingly, the provincial Act of Incorporation under which Hamilton's Sisters of St. Joseph's orphan asylum was administered created a body politic of the Mother Superior, four particular sisters, and "such other persons as shall ... become members of the said Association." This corporation was empowered to hold and sell property, sue and be sued, as well as make and repeal rules governing their association.[8] The 1864 act that incorporated Hamilton's Children's Industrial School also created a legal entity composed of female managers and invested it with all of the usual corporate capacities, except that it could only hold real property amounting to less than two thousand dollars.[9]

The HOA/LBS's act also subjected the association's administration to the regulatory gaze of both governmental bodies and the public. Incorporation required the Society to keep a list of all subscribers, hold annual meetings after "due notice" given in a local newspaper, and send "Annual Returns to the Governor ... shewing [sic] the amount of their receipts and expenditure ... and of the real and personal estate held and enjoyed by the said Corporation."[10] These technologies of government reimposed male and state authority, mitigated female administrative control, and simultaneously elevated this mid-nineteenth-century child welfare charity to the status of a legitimated, state-sanctioned institution.[11]

While marginalizing women in several respects, these parliamentary acts delegated female managers with considerable powers over orphaned *and* dependent children. The HOA's Committee of Management was authorized to "send out to service, and apprentice thereto, or to any healthy trade or business, all youths, male or female, having the protection and aid of the said Institution, to such person or persons, and upon such terms, as to the said Ladies' Committee of Management may seem fit and proper." The committee could "enter into and make with any person or persons with whom such youths may be placed ... articles of apprenticeship and agreement: and that such articles of agreement may be enforced as well by action at law."[12]

The act placed few limits on the Committee of Management's power to apprentice children, which abrogated the guardianship rights of any parent whose child came under "the protection and aid" of the asylum. The power to apprentice delegated to mid-nineteenth-century child welfare institutions such as the Hamilton Orphan Asylum was generally consistent with a law passed in Canada West in 1851. The Apprentices and Minors Act permitted any parent, guardian, or other person "having the care or charge of" a child fourteen years of age or older to apprentice them. It also allowed a consenting child of any age to be bound by a public official if the child "had been orphaned or deserted, if his parents or guardians had been committed to gaol, or if he was 'dependent upon any public charity for support.'"[13]

The legal principle behind these acts reflected British Poor Law practice of involuntary apprenticeship, which assumed that "dependency abrogated common-law rights."[14] In the United States, during the nineteenth century, several state judiciaries upheld "involuntary indenture," wherein dependent parents who were unable to support their child had their guardianship rights annulled by the state.[15] The Hamilton Orphan Asylum and institutions like it were delegated the power of *parens patriae* – the right of the state to assume custodial control of children – over poor and dependent parents in particular.

The HOA/LBS's Act of Incorporation also reflects a principle first introduced into US law in the *Ex parte Crouse* ruling (1838) by the Pennsylvania Supreme Court, which upheld the right of the state to remove children from homes that deviated from "the republican ideal of a socially beneficial family."[16] The republican vision of family, according to Michael Grossberg, was "a collection of individuals each with his or her own needs and rights."[17] Therefore, those families in which each individual's needs and rights – to decent food, clothing, and shelter, for example – were not protected could be subjected to state intervention. This ruling set a legal precedent that protected individual rights within the family rather than privileging patriarchal sovereignty over dependants. In other words, this law heralded an ideological shift that would ultimately lead to the wholesale institutionalization of modern, liberal familial ideals.[18]

The HOA's Committee of Management's power to apprentice any child admitted into the asylum had significant consequences for those with parents. Although nineteenth-century childcare institutions were often called "orphan asylums," many of the children admitted had at least one living parent. Timothy Hasci found that most children in US asylums had one living parent and, as mortality rates fell over the course of the nineteenth century, the percentage of asylum children with families increased.[19] According to Charlotte Neff, of 469 children admitted into the HOA between 1848 and 1875, 43 percent had one parent living.[20]

Even higher proportions of "half-orphans" were admitted into the Toronto Protestant Orphans' Home, Kingston Orphans' Home, and Ottawa Protestant Orphans' Home.[21] According to Patricia T. Rooke and R.L. Schnell, the majority of inmates at the Church of England Orphans' and Widows' Aid Society in St. John's, established in 1855, were fatherless children with mothers who could not provide for them.[22] Seventy percent of the children cared for by Montreal's Ladies' Benevolent Society had one parent living, most of whom were women. Although Montreal's Protestant Orphan Asylum had an "orphans-only policy," only 64 percent of admissions were full orphans.[23]

Paradoxically, the HOA/LBS Act of Incorporation granted the female Committee of Management authority over some people's children that they, as mothers, did not have over their own. Throughout most of the nineteenth century in Britain and parts of North America, all legitimate children were legal wards of their fathers. Laws of coverture defined maternal guardianship only insofar as a married woman acted as her husband's agent.[24] Although guardianship of children could devolve to mothers by testamentary action of the father, a widow could not exercise full rights of guardianship over her children without restrictions in Ontario until 1877.[25] In 1855, widowed mothers in Canada West were granted guardianship rights over children under twelve, however. In Britain, widowed mothers were not granted full rights of guardianship until 1886.[26]

Most nineteenth-century Ontario asylums' and children's homes' Acts of Incorporation included some proviso that empowered the institutions' managers to apprentice children. Those who did not have this power apparently circumvented the problem by apprenticing children through other institutions.[27] Interestingly, in the case of the orphan asylum administered by Hamilton's Sisters of St. Joseph, no such provisions for the guardianship of orphans or destitute children were included in its Act of Incorporation.[28] Extant evidence shows, nonetheless, that children from the institution were indeed "placed out" and "adopted in families."[29] In contrast, the 1864 act that incorporated the Children's Industrial School of Hamilton, originally organized as the Girls' Home, included an article that granted the institution's managers "such power as [the children's] parents or guardians would have or might exercise."[30] This was particularly significant because the Girls' Home's explicit purpose was to care for children with living parents.

Despite their legal prerogative to do so, the HOA/LBS Committee of Management did not ordinarily demand that parents give up their guardianship rights permanently. For most children, the Hamilton Orphan Asylum functioned, in the words of Hasci, as a "protective" rather than "isolating" institution. Protective asylums attempted insofar as possible to remove children from the outside world but willingly returned children to their natural families. Isolating asylums, in contrast, sometimes went to great lengths to separate children and their parents. Managers of isolating institutions were often determined to break the child's bond with his or her heritage, particularly in the case of religious difference. Hasci also notes that an asylum might be protective for some children and isolating for others.[31] The HOA appears to fit into this hybrid model since some children were willingly returned to their parent or family, whereas others, sometimes Roman Catholic children, were not.

Despite welfare historians' traditional emphasis on social control, many others have recognized that social welfare institutions, despite punitive or exclusionary policies, did in fact help some marginal families in their struggle for survival.[32] Hasci argues that "more than most social welfare institutions, orphan asylums performed the duty that their clientele wished them to by helping poor families survive harsh times through temporarily caring for children."[33] He contends that "the widespread belief that children and parents should be kept together if possible, and that poor parents might also be 'worthy' parents, was not simply a product of the early twentieth century." By the 1860s, many asylum managers in the United States had abandoned the view that poor families were unworthy of aid.[34]

Bruce Bellingham takes a slightly different tack and argues that, "in the context of their needs and available options, surrendering parents actually had an interest in filial discontinuity."[35] In other words, despite historians' portrayals of asylum managers as imposing policies that countered the interests of poor parents, he found that child welfare institutions in nineteenth-century America "often reached some expedient accommodation with client goals and interests."[36]

In Hamilton, poor families found themselves in need for myriad reasons. For instance, international immigration and high rates of mobility and transiency left more people without extensive familial networks to bridge themselves through difficult times.[37] Michael Katz discovered high rates of mobility especially amongst the poor in mid-nineteenth-century Hamilton. Transiency, Katz proposed, was "a key feature" of Hamilton's social structure in this era.[38] Also, with few opportunities for child or female labour, reliance upon a single male wage made the working family economy especially precarious. Peter Mandler observes that in the "single-industry city," such as iron and steel towns like Hamilton, "where neither child nor female labor was in demand," families struggled to keep the family wage above subsistence at the best of times.[39] Single parents who brought their children to the Hamilton Orphan Asylum invariably faced what Mandler calls a "critical life situation" that forced them to seek charitable assistance.[40]

During the mid-nineteenth century, the Hamilton Orphan Asylum and other childcare institutions like it regularly offered temporary custodial care for children with living relatives. For example, Hamilton's St. Mary's Orphan Asylum reported that, in 1864, the institution admitted forty-two children "at the request of parents or friends" and several others were "taken away by their parents or guardians."[41] Between 1848 and 1875, the Hamilton Orphan Asylum admitted 114 children whose mothers were alive, which represented 24 percent of its total admissions.[42] In December 1863, for example, the Committee of Management discharged "a little boy named Whiteside, who had been given a temporary home in the Asylum," to his mother.[43] In March 1867, the Committee of Management released William Smith to his mother "as she was recovered and able to take care of him."[44]

Asylum managers sometimes opted to provide mothers with outdoor relief rather than take children out of their homes, a strategy that presaged widows' benefits or mothers' allowances. In June 1868, Mrs. Bale, "a widow ... in bad health," requested that her "very young" children be admitted into the asylum. The Committee of Management increased her monthly allowance from the visiting society funds instead.[45] According to its 1865 annual report, the Sisters of St. Mary's Orphan Asylum in Hamilton also distributed outdoor relief to seventy-two families whose children "frequently found a refuge in the hospitable walls of the Asylum."[46]

Single fathers also sought the HOA's assistance when they could not care for their children. Ninety children admitted into the asylum prior to 1875 had living fathers.[47] Margaret Stein's father, for example, removed her from the asylum in August 1854 after he recovered from an illness.[48] In January 1872, Edith Sharp was admitted into the asylum and discharged to her father in April.[49] In July, however, Edith's father admitted her again and negotiated an agreement with the Committee of Management that he would reclaim his daughter in six months.[50]

In a few cases, the orphan asylum also boarded children whose parent was able to pay for their maintenance. In December 1868, Mrs. Farrar agreed to pay the two dollar per month fee so that her little girl could stay in the asylum.[51] In April 1865, another child was admitted whose mother also paid two dollars a month for board.[52] Hasci found that many nineteenth-century US asylums also accepted boarders.[53] In British North America, the Kingston Orphan Asylum admitted fee-paying children for temporary residential accommodation, as did the Toronto Protestant Orphan Home, Toronto Girls' Home, Halifax Infants' Home, and Saint John Protestant Orphan Asylum.[54] In Hamilton, the Children's Industrial School's 1865 annual report recorded an income of ninety-five dollars from parents for their children's board.[55]

These examples demonstrate that the Hamilton Orphan Asylum and other mid-nineteenth-century child welfare institutions played an important role in some lone parents' attempts to maintain their children and ultimately keep their families intact. The Committee of Management did not encourage these struggling parents to give their children up permanently; nor did the committee record in its private records any negative judgments or punitive actions taken against lone mothers and fathers. The committee's treatment of these cases also betrays an assumption that these particular children were best raised by their parents and in their own homes.

Although the HOA often admitted children with one living parent and over the years also admitted children with two parents living, the Committee of Management sometimes objected to the admission of certain children with living parents. In several cases, these were children sent "by Mayor's order," for which the City paid a fee. In June 1857, for example, the committee sent a resolution to the mayor's office stating that "as the greater number of those who are admitted by orders from the Mayor have either one or both parents living, it has become a matter of necessity to restrict the Orphan Asylum to the special object for which it was instituted."[56] In October 1858, the committee reiterated their objection to accepting children with parents sent in by the mayor. The HOA/LBS's twelfth annual report, which was published in Hamilton's newspapers, explained that no child would be accepted by mayor's order "who was not given up entirely to the control of the Ladies Committee of Management."[57] In July 1867, the visitors reported that Henry and Walter Hattersbey were "brought by their mother" to the asylum "on Mayor's order."[58] The committee refused to accept the Hattersbey children and "another boy McAuley" since the children each had two living parents. According to their letter to the mayor, the committee took this action, "not wishing except in cases of strongest necessity to encourage the giving up of children by their parents; and desiring to preserve to their Institution, its character of an Orphan Asylum." The committee also directed Samuel Wilson, the asylum's superintendent, to "request the Mayor not to give orders to children in future except on personal application from the Ladies."[59]

This evidence suggests that the Committee of Management could invoke the asylum's status as an orphans' institution and "not wishing ... to encourage the giving up to children by their parents" to prevent the admission of particular parents' children, while using their discretion to admit other children with parents when disposed to do so. On what criteria these decisions were made is unclear. The more important point, however, is that the committee was at liberty to judge which parents and children were and were not eligible for its services.

The Committee of Management did not, at least in this latter case, turn children without responsible guardians out onto the streets. In August, the committee "order[ed] the removal of the Hattersbey boys, and also little McAuley." This order was apparently not enforced, and the boys were "retained in the Asylum." James McAuley was dismissed a few days later for "breaking the rules of the Asylum" and "endeavouring to corrupt the other boys." Although the child was sent back to his mother, the superintendent later found McAuley "wandering in the streets" and brought him back to the asylum.[60] The committee did not send the Hattersbey boys back to their parents either. In 1870, nearly two and a half years later, the visitors reported, "Henry and Walter Hattersby [sic] were on 14th Feb[rua]ry taken from the Asylum by their mother."[61] Despite the rigidity of the committee's official position vis-à-vis the mayor, the managers sometimes had difficulty actually enforcing their own policy decisions.

Although the Committee of Management usually returned children to their parents' custody, in some instances they did try to compel parents to surrender their children to the orphan asylum permanently. In October 1865, the committee admitted two children whose mother was "entirely unable to support them" and "thought to be a most unprincipled woman." The managers accepted these children into the asylum only after their mother agreed "to give up all claim on them and interest in them."[62] Some parents refused to accept these terms.[63] In November 1858, for example, Jerome Cornell was admitted into the asylum on the condition that he was "given up by his mother entirely to the charge of the Ladies Board of Management."[64] The committee attempted to get Mary Keagan, Jerome's mother, to "sign a paper giving up all control over him." She would not assent and took the child out of the asylum.[65]

The Committee of Management sometimes returned children to their parents even after they had signed away their parental rights. William Liddel was discharged back to his father who, according to the committee's reports, was "a man of intemperate habits" and "totally neglected" his children, in December 1869, two years after he gave up control over his son.[66] Although Mrs. Farrar "signed a paper in presence of the Ladies renouncing all further claim upon [her son]" in December 1868, William Farrar was returned to his mother's custody in September 1870.[67]

In the face of parental resistance, the committee often opted to re-establish families rather than execute its prerogative over children given up by their parents. In her analysis of nineteenth-century Protestant Children's Homes in Ontario, Neff found that this was usually the case.[68] Montreal's Protestant Orphan Asylum required some parents to "legally bind their children to the society" but, according to Janice Harvey, these were "rarely implemented."[69] Carolyn Lawes also found, in her study of the Children's Friend Society of Worchester, Massachusetts, female managers were reluctant to exert their legal authority over children when parents attempted to re-establish their guardianship.[70] This evidence contradicts historians who have accepted later "child-savers" rhetoric, which discredited mid-nineteenth-century childcare institutions as "too ready to label parents as worthless and undeserving and their children as neglected and in need of protection."[71]

Indeed, in the case of William Liddel, his father's "intemperate" habits and neglectful parenting were not sufficient justifications for the Committee of Management to retain the child. In this instance, the committee privileged a doctrine of parental rights – and insisted that Mr. Liddel bear the burden of parental responsibility – rather than intervene on behalf of what may have been this child's "best interest." The committee's unwillingness to retain children even when their parent did not show suitable regard for his or her child's well-being betrays a conservatism that legal scholars have explained was rooted in "a hierarchic conception of society."[72]

This notion of family held paternal rights as sacrosanct and regarded the natural family as an indivisible whole governed by a divine law of order. Children were regarded as "dependent, subordinate beings, [and] assets of estates in which fathers had a vested right."[73] According to Constance Backhouse, throughout most of the nineteenth century, the Ontario judiciary tended to "preserve patriarchal control" in custody law cases and showed "a reluctance to undermine the father's authority in the family."[74]

The Committee of Management demonstrated no preference for preserving paternal rather than maternal rights. In 1847, prior to the LBS's incorporation, the Society received a request from the city police to care for a baby whose mother was "so much given to intoxication, that the life of the child was in jeopardy." This request came in the second year of the LBS's institutional history, when the Committee of Management was aware that its decisions would set precedents for the Society's future operations. The LBS's managers decided that "to take the child would be an encouragement to interference in parents, especially mothers, and however the Society may feel for the infant, they cannot as a public body take it under their care."[75] In this case, the LBS refused to act in what may very well have been the child's best interest and specifically rejected the notion that the Society or the police ought to interfere in maternal rights or responsibilities.

In a few instances, the Committee of Management did, however, go to great lengths to keep children away from their natural parent. In 1879, the Committee of Management received several requests from Mrs. Brule to remove her daughter, Harriet, from the asylum. The committee refused to give up the girl and recorded that Mrs. Brule's "character is not good and no reliance can be placed on her statements."[76] Later that month, when Mrs. Brule continued to harass the committee to return her daughter, the managers refused again on the grounds that "the account given of her by the Chief of Police ... was a very bad one," and he advised the committee to "have nothing more to say to her and to keep the child from her."[77]

In another example, in March 1862, the Committee of Management had noted with "regret" that Mrs. Latimer had not "avail[ed] herself of the privilege" of admitting her children into the asylum. Apparently, Mrs. Latimer had "given them to the nuns," even though, according to the committee, "her husband on his deathbed made her promise that they should be brought up Protestants."[78] In November 1863, however, the committee was informed that Mrs. Latimer was in hospital and had left her three children "quite without a protector or guardian." The children were admitted into the Hamilton Orphan Asylum when their mother agreed to "give them up entirely" to the committee.[79] Three years later, Mrs. Latimer attempted to reclaim her daughter, Mary Jane, from the place to which she had been apprenticed. The HOA/LBS's secretary, Harriet Juson, reported that Mary Jane's "worthless mother had found her out" and was giving her master and mistress "much annoyance." Juson subsequently wrote to Mary Jane's master with instructions to "try to return her to the Asylum, rather than she should be taken by her mother."[80] In the committee's estimation, Mary Jane's best interests were served in her current position rather than in the care of her "worthless mother." In this case, religious prejudice and a desire to preserve Mrs. Latimer's children from a Roman Catholic upbringing very likely influenced the Committee of Management's course of action.

In these instances, the committee did exercise its power to break up natural families. The HOA's Act of Incorporation ultimately authorized it to assume guardianship rights over children with living parents. The committee could also rely upon the support and cooperation of other legitimated authorities, including the police. In this way, the asylum's managers were exercising an authority, bestowed upon them by the state, to act *either* to protect parental rights *or* to act in a child's best interest as they saw fit.

According to Grossberg, over the course of the nineteenth century in the United States, the "best interest of the child" doctrine facilitated state intervention into families via the principle of *parens patriae,* while it simultaneously opened the way for the legal protection of mother's rights. American custody law gradually accommodated the idea that a father's custody power was "a trust tied to his responsibility as a guardian."[81] This shift meant that "courts could award custody by examining a child's interests rather than by merely assessing the legitimacy of parental claims."[82]

Backhouse has argued that state intervention on behalf of children's best interest did not "emerge with any strength in Canada until after the turn of the century." The first judicial decision in Ontario that she found that "illustrated a departure from the notion of quasi-property paternal rights over children" and focused instead on the child's best interest was in 1881.[83] She claimed that it was not until the early twentieth century that "a trend" emerged toward granting charitable institutions custody over abandoned children.[84] While certainly the volume and numbers of interventions into parental authority increased in the late nineteenth and early twentieth century, the case of the HOA provides evidence that this trend had its beginnings in a much earlier period. It also suggests that custody law probably lagged behind both ideology and practice.

The case of the Hamilton Orphan Asylum illuminates several critical relationships between family and institution in this mid-nineteenth-century community. The HOA offered families, in particular those headed by lone parents, an alternative similar to that provided by kin and neighbours in other contexts. In Hamilton, high rates of migration, lack of child and female employment, and a patriarchal family ethic conspired against the subsistence economy of single women with children. To a degree and for some families, the asylum ameliorated this "critical life situation."

While the HOA's conceptualization of the family as a site of mutual obligation and the best environment in which to raise children militated against philanthropic abduction, a doctrine of best interest had the opposite effect. The subjectivity of best interest meant that private associations, such as the HOA/LBS, were granted tremendous power by the state to naturalize and institutionalize its own conceptualization of ideal familial relations and parental behaviour.

Since the HOA regulated, intervened, and participated in the maintenance of the families with which it dealt, this conceptualization of family was neither private nor ideologically neutral. The HOA was empowered to establish a code of familial conduct and, in turn, hold others accountable to it. Parental failure to comply with this code justified removing their children to the care of others. In other words, private relations were transformed into public responsibility. Although some parents were able to make their needs congruent with the services offered by the HOA through – albeit unequal – negotiation, a particular notion of proper familial arrangements could always be used to subvert parents' coping strategies and legitimize their disempowerment.

6
Institutional Care, Adoption, and Apprenticeship

THE HAMILTON ORPHAN Asylum had three different means by which it provided for children: institutional care, adoption, and apprenticeship. The first involved boarding children within the asylum; although institutionalization was not the Committee of Management's preferred method of childcare, most children spent at least some time in the orphanage. The latter two options involved sending children out to live with a family, which was intended to provide children with responsible guardians during their growing-up years. The committee's decisions and policies regarding childcare strategies reveal particular assumptions about the institution's roles and responsibilities, as well as attitudes about children and the family.

Institutional Care

The very notion of an "asylum" rested on the principle of environmentalism. Indeed, the proliferation of orphans' asylums in the United States, Britain, and Canada during the nineteenth century can be explained on this principle alone.[1] Orphan asylums were seen as fundamentally different from the workhouse or house of refuge. While the latter institutions were conceived largely as warehouses for society's dregs, the former were meant to provide an ideal environment. To use a metaphor often engaged by child savers in the later nineteenth century, the orphan asylum was to children what a greenhouse was for young, tender plants: a sheltering place to be protected and nurtured so that they might grow into strong and healthy adults.[2]

The HOA/LBS's annual reports often argued that, once removed from a vicious and demoralizing environment, children could be entirely reclaimed and transformed into respectable citizens. The 1862 report described orphan children "found in a state of great destitution in the coldest season of the year," "emaciated and ... neglected" or "taken from the very depth of degradation" who were "now all filling respectable positions in life."[3] According to the annual reports, these children "could only have become outcasts upon the world, a misery to themselves and to all in contact with them" if they had been deprived of the asylum's benefits.[4] These statements betray the committee's sense that its work with children was especially efficacious, as well as its desire to convince supporters of the asylum's service to the public good.

The notion that a proper environment could preserve children from future immorality and idleness did not lead managers to favour institutional care over placements in private homes, however. Although later commentators, particularly J.J. Kelso, criticized nineteenth-century asylums for institutionalizing children, Charlotte Neff argues that, generally speaking, only "a minority of children experienced long-term institutional care" in Protestant children's homes in Ontario. Depending on the institution, "only one-tenth to one-third stayed three years or more."[5] She also notes that most of the 6 to 15 percent of children who stayed in Ontario Protestant children's homes for five years or longer had "significant special needs."[6]

The Hamilton Orphan Asylum was no exception. Neff calculated that between 1848 and 1869 the median number of months children resided in the asylum was seven. Thereafter, children stayed somewhat longer: between 1870 and 1879, the median was sixteen months; between 1880 and 1886, the median was fourteen months.[7] The Committee of Management's minute books also provide evidence that children who stayed long periods in the asylum were usually suffering from chronic illness or disability.[8]

The most basic tenet of the committee's childcare policy was that children were best raised in a home or homelike atmosphere. Asylum managers sought insofar as possible to replicate their own assumptions about what constituted an appropriate and well-managed home for these children. This was a family-centred space that necessarily included a father and mother figure, in which children would receive kindness and discipline, a religious and elementary education, as well as opportunities for play and work.

Children who were admitted between the ages of five and eleven received boarding, care, and an education in the asylum.[9] These children lived together in the house, along with those younger and older children who were eligible for adoption or apprenticeship but had not been placed in other homes. Between July 6, 1848, and December 31, 1869, 463 children were admitted into the Orphan Asylum.[10] As few as thirteen but as many as forty-eight children lived in the asylum at any one time.[11] On average, it was home to about thirty children.[12] The matron and superintendent, their biological children, as well as staff members, who sometimes had children of their own, also lived in the house.[13]

When the asylum was first established in 1848, the managers hired Emma Wilson as the resident matron at a rate of £25 per year. The following year they also engaged her husband, Samuel, as superintendent. Surprisingly, since women's work was ordinarily undervalued and underpaid relative to men's, he was also paid £25 per year.[14] Together, husband and wife taught the children and managed the asylum's day-to-day activities until their retirement in 1879.[15]

The matron's and superintendent's work was, not surprisingly, segregated according to traditional gender roles. Emma Wilson oversaw domestic affairs within the asylum, which included managing a staff of servants. The matron was also responsible for the general regulation of the household, such as running or overseeing the affairs of the kitchen, laundry, pantries, bedrooms, and so on. She monitored and occasionally purchased supplies for the kitchen and household and was generally responsible for the children's well-being. In addition to teaching, she nursed children when they were sick, bathed them, cared for infants, and trained older girls to help around the house.

Samuel Wilson, to whom the asylum's visitors and Committee of Management referred simply as "Wilson," fulfilled teaching duties and maintained the house, storerooms, cellar, stables, barn, sheds, and yard. A garden, orchard, and honey bees also occupied a good deal of Samuel Wilson's time, especially in the spring and fall. Wilson handled most of the purchasing for the asylum, made recommendations to the committee about repairs and alterations needed in and around the house, and kept records of children admitted and discharged. The Committee of Management exercised authority over all of Wilson's duties, which included carrying out its decisions concerning the admission and discharge of children. Samuel Wilson was also instructed to find apprenticeships for specific children, to make inquiries about parents, masters, or children, to check up on children apprenticed, collect overdue accounts from masters, and contact potential masters or adopting parents with the committee's decisions on their requests for children.

Like most nineteenth-century orphan asylums, the Committee of Management attempted to create a "homelike atmosphere" for children. Visitors, chosen from the Society's membership to inspect the asylum on one-month rotations, submitted reports that were read out at the Society's bimonthly meetings. These reports commonly referred to the asylum as a "home" and its residents as a "family." In December 1866, Lydia Jackson and Mary Bickle remarked upon "the homelike influence by which they [the children] are surrounded." They expressed the "hope" that the asylum was thereby "silently moulding them [the children] for walks of future usefulness."[16] Nearly ten years later, Sarah Winer and Mary Bickle reported to the Society that they had "found the same order, cleanliness and cheerfulness which has for so many years made the Asylum a true home for the little ones committed to our care."[17] The visitors clearly assumed that a homelike environment would benefit the children and help ensure that they would grow up into functional adults.

A homelike atmosphere necessarily included parents, and the visitors expected Samuel and Emma Wilson to act *in loco parentis* for the children in their care. Visitors also praised affectionate, loving, and indulgent behaviour by the Wilsons. In September 1859, Sarah Winer and Marie Brown reported they "always found Mr and Mrs Wilson ... apparently anxious to do everything for the comfort, happiness and improvement of the children."[18] In July 1862, for example, the superintendent and matron took six boys and some of the girls to Oaklands for a picnic and provided them with refreshments and fishing rods for the boys. Mrs. Walker and Sarah Winer reported to the committee their "gratification ... to see the kind watchful care bestowed upon those little ones by those who had the charge of them."[19] The Wilsons' behaviour as kindly surrogate parents was frequently noted by the visitors and was evidently regarded as both appropriate and necessary for the well-being of asylum children.

The Committee of Management expected Emma Wilson, in particular, to fill the role of supportive and tender maternal figure. Visitors often remarked upon Mrs. Wilson's "true motherly kindness."[20] In June 1868, Susan Geddes and Sarah Winer recorded that "they cannot conclude [their report] without bearing testimony to the untiring zeal of Mrs Wilson – were the children her own she could not be more kind and motherly in all her dealings with them."[21] In April 1876, Mrs. Bickle and Mrs. Street commented on "how much [they] were impressed by Mrs Wilsons [sic] tender motherly care of the sick ones and their love for her as manifested by their ready obedience to her wishes."[22] The visitors ascribed to Emma Wilson a special capacity for childcare, nurture, and domestic virtue. Historians have noted that over the course of the nineteenth century the importance of maternal stewardship over private life increased, which tended to elevate and idealize women's role in the home.[23] This shift is clearly evident in the visitors' expectations of the matron.

The Committee of Management also expected the asylum to approximate the routine and discipline of a well-regulated, middle-class household.[24] The asylum children's lives revolved around school, work, and recreation. According to the Orphan Asylum's "Rules for Daily Occupation," children rose at six, washed, dressed, made their beds, tidied their rooms, said their prayers, and ate breakfast. From eight o'clock until nine, the younger children played and older ones assisted Mrs. Wilson with house duties. At nine o'clock, school began with prayer and reading scriptures, and lessons continued until noon. From twelve until two o'clock, the children ate dinner and worked or played. School resumed at two and continued until five o'clock. The time between five and six o'clock was available for play or work. Supper was served at six, and at seven o'clock the children prepared for bed.[25] Interestingly, this routine was virtually indistinguishable from that of the Boston Female Asylum.[26] Routines such as these were not unique to child-saving institutions either. Sophia MacNab, the daughter of Hamilton politician and HOA/LBS trustee Allan MacNab, recorded a very similar schedule in her childhood diary, which she and her sister were meant to follow.[27]

Children's education was accorded a great deal of importance by the Committee of Management and visitors, which seems consistent with other childcare institutions' policies and practices. Neff found that all of the nineteenth-century child welfare institutions that she studied provided children with some education.[28] She has argued that education provided to dependent children in orphan asylums was "at the heart of the mandate of these homes."[29]

Educational schemes in Canada during the formative era of public education were based on the notion that schools could mitigate negative influences on children, particularly from their families. Susan Houston and Alison Prentice observe that builders of the public education system espoused the following sentiments: "Malleable and terribly vulnerable to influence, any given child faced two possibilities. If exposed to evil or allowed to remain idle, the potential for sin, economic ruin, or political degeneracy was great. But if sufficiently schooled, there was the real possibility of individual improvement and, ultimately, moral, political, and economic salvation."[30] These same assumptions appear to have animated the Hamilton Orphan Asylum's school policies and practices.

In 1848, when the Society established a day school in connection with its orphanage, the school was intended to provide education to poor children in the community as well as those domiciled in the asylum. Any child over the age of two was eligible for admission to the day school, provided that they were "clean, their clothes clean and decently mended, and their hair cut and combed." Children from town were required to pay a weekly fee of a penny, except for "cases of the very poor." One child could be sponsored by each annual subscriber to the Society and admitted for free "after due investigation by the Benevolent Society Visitor, and the Committee being satisfied they are *bona fide* cases of charity."[31] The asylum's school for resident children admitted day scholars until 1853, when Hamilton's Central School opened. At that time, the Committee of Management decided that its school was rendered superfluous since the Central School offered "a free and liberal education for all."[32] Thereafter, the Wilsons instructed children resident in the asylum only.

Emma and Samuel Wilson taught the children arithmetic, writing, and reading in the asylum's schoolroom. Later on, geography and singing were added to the curriculum. According to Houston and Prentice, a common school education in early nineteenth-century Ontario was usually confined to the three Rs, while some schools also included grammar and geography.[33] Timothy Hasci found that mid-nineteenth-century orphan asylums in the United States usually taught reading, writing, spelling, geography, and arithmetic, in addition to religious lessons.[34] Children in Montreal's Protestant Orphan Asylum received instructions in "spelling, reading, writing, arithmetic, geography, and grammar."[35] At the Toronto Widows' and Orphans' Asylum, children were taught reading, spelling, writing, arithmetic, sewing, and knitting.[36]

The Hamilton Orphan Asylum's school's management adhered closely to educational legislation in the province and generally conformed to norms and standards that governed other educational facilities. This may have been at least in part owing to the influence of one of the LBS's three vice presidents, Mary Armstrong Ryerson, whose husband was Canada West's chief superintendent of education, Egerton Ryerson.[37] The Committee of Management's "Rules for School Visitors," for example, emulated the provincial education department's "General Regulations and Instructions," which were established to administer legislation passed in 1846. Both visitors, in the case of the committee's rules, and superintendents, in the case of the provincial regulations, were instructed to offer advice to teachers only in private, to uphold the authority of the teacher while in the classroom, and to act courteously in the execution of their administrative duties.[38] Such instructions were typical.[39] This is yet another example of how the Society attempted to make its work consistent with values to which other public bodies and institutions adhered.

Visitors participated directly in asylum children's education by assisting in the classroom and examining pupils' progress. In March 1860, Jane McLaren and Mrs. Bellhouse noted that the children were making good progress in their lessons. They listened to the children read and "questioned them and were much pleased with the readiness and intelligence of their answers, evincing the care and pains Mr. Wilson takes that they may *thoroughly* understand the sense of what they learn."[40] These women expressed a preference for an interactive learning style rather than rote memorization, which reflected mid-century educational reforms that were gaining popularity in Ontario schools.[41]

The Orphan Asylum's school was also subject to a rule that made it consistent with an amendment to the province's Common School Act of 1841 and the Hincks Act of 1843. The latter amendment attempted to placate the parents of Roman Catholic children who opposed bible reading in the schools.[42] In 1848, notably prior to the controversy that arose in 1852 about the asylum proselytizing Roman Catholic orphans, the Committee of Management decided that "the scriptures shall be daily read in the school, but that no child whose parents may object, be obliged to study or read them."[43] This rule did not, of course, protect the religious freedom of children without parents to object.

Despite the Hamilton Orphan Asylum's purported nonsectarianism, religious education played a centrally important role in its curriculum, as was the case in most nineteenth-century schools.[44] Hasci observed that in the United States religious training was "at the core of most asylum managers' thinking for over a century."[45] During the mid-nineteenth century, some evangelical Protestants in English Canada endorsed the notion that moral and ethical teachings early in life could protect children from sin. For these evangelicals, the theological doctrine of infant depravity was abandoned and replaced with childhood innocence and purity.[46] Education could, therefore, help preserve children's sinless state, rendering reformation later on unnecessary. Although this vision of childhood may not have been universally accepted until the late nineteenth century, there is evidence that the HOA/LBS adopted this philosophy of childhood decades earlier.

The notion of childhood innocence is, for example, evinced clearly in the orphan asylum's school prayer. Teachers and children began their prayer, which was recited each morning, with the passage, "suffer little children to come unto me and, forbid them not, regard with thy favour every effort to bring up children in the nurture and admonition of the Lord." The prayer asked that children "remember their creator in the days of their youth" and "that early seeking Jesus the Saviour they may early find him." An appeal was made that the children "be trained up in the way they should go, and when they are old never depart from it."[47] This prayer suggests that the asylum's managers envisioned themselves providing children with a proper moral and religious environment in the expectation that this upbringing would protect them from sin and degradation later in life.

The moral principles and religious training imparted by scriptural study was particularly valued by the asylum visitors. In June 1871, Lydia Jackson and Mrs. Walker observed a class repeat a portion of scripture "without one mistake" and "on being questioned by one of the visitors on the various portions ... were delighted with the intelligent answers they each gave."[48] In June 1876, Sarah Winer and Mary Bickle reported that they observed the "diligent attention of the children to their lessons and the progress they are making especially in the study of the Bible and as we listened to the simple earnest words of Mrs Wilson we felt that such teaching must leave an impression which will remain with them through all their lives."[49] The reproduction of evangelical Protestant values and ethics, as well as training children "up in the way they should go," were clearly integral to the orphan asylum's mandate.

In addition to the children's moral and secular education, the matron and superintendent were also charged with practical training. Work was clearly demarcated by gender. Boys assisted Samuel Wilson in duties out of doors, such as yard work, gardening, animal husbandry, carpentry, and general maintenance of the house and outbuildings. Girls helped Emma Wilson and the domestic servants with cleaning, scrubbing, washing dishes, sewing, and laundry, and in the nursery.

Domestic work was deemed particularly important training for girls. In March 1860, Jane McLaren and Mrs. Bellhouse commented in their report that sewing was "a most important part of their [the girls'] education and cannot fail to prove most valuable to them in after life."[50] Elizabeth Thomas, the HOA/LBS's president, suggested in September 1865, "the elder girls be taught to assist more in the housework, and in washing and ironing, so as to fit them for service."[51] Since, according to Hamilton's 1861 census, 59 percent of women who worked were employed as domestic servants and 14 percent as seamstresses, milliners, and dressmakers, training in these skills was highly practical.[52]

For women, employment did not, however, lead to independence. Women in Hamilton who worked for wages were usually poor.[53] Unlike boys, who were trained in the asylum and as apprentices for occupations that could provide them with a livelihood sufficient to support themselves, such as farming or trades, women were trained for dependence. In this way, the orphan asylum's practical education directly perpetuated patriarchal family relations. Girls were expected to work in economically marginal jobs that made marriage a financial necessity, while boys were given legitimate opportunities for economic independence.

The Hamilton Orphan Asylum did not, unlike some other childcare institutions, rely heavily upon the children's labour. The asylum always employed a full staff of servants. The Halifax Protestant Orphan's Home, in contrast, operated "entirely ... on the children's contribution to household tasks ... with no other domestic help from its founding in 1857 until 1871."[54] Hasci notes that, in general, "daily chores to perform was [sic] one of the most common aspects of orphans asylum life across time, region, and type of orphan asylum."[55] At the Montreal Protestant Orphan Asylum, for example, children did most of the light work around the institution.[56]

In Hamilton, the Committee of Management and visitors expected that asylum children ought to have opportunities for enjoyment and recreation during their growing-up years. Hasci observed that even the earliest American orphan asylums also allowed children some time to play. By the 1850s, "asylum managers were beginning to view children's play as an important aspect of growing up."[57] Harriet Juson and Mrs. H.B. McDonald reported in January 1867 that, on their visits, they "generally found [the children] in happy groups engaged about their toys."[58] In 1869, Elizabeth McQuesten and Clara Ormiston commented that the "children were all made happy by Christmas gifts a quantity of toys and books having been bought for them and the usual bountiful provision made for their Christmas dinner."[59] Mrs. Sutherland and Mrs. Walker noted in July 1859 that the annual summer holiday was "much enjoyed by the children during the warm weather, and undoubtedly contributed to their health."[60] In July 1864, Mrs. Sutherland reported the "children have been enjoying their summer holidays, and Mr Wilson has been so kind as to take them once to hear the Band, which pleased them very much. They have been feasting on the fruits of the garden and appear unusually well and happy."[61]

An emphasis upon holidays, toys, and entertainments demonstrates that the Committee of Management and visitors shared a specific set of domestic values that were focused on children's well-being and oriented daily life around the family.[62]

Despite their expectations, however, children in the asylum were not uniformly happy or content. This is best evinced by several children who attempted to escape their "home" in the asylum. In August 1867, two boys ran away. According to Lydia Jackson and Mrs. Walker, Samuel Wilson made a "diligent search" and gave "word to the Police to look out for them." Eventually, the boys returned and were "taken before the committee and reprimanded; promising not again to commit a similar fault."[63] The next month the visitors were still having trouble with the boys. Susan Geddes and Sarah Winer reported that "some of the boys have been troublesome in inducing some of the little boys to run away that they might be sent to find them. They have been punished but do not seem to feel it much."[64] In November 1868, two boys "named Wesley and McFetteridge left the Asylum one morning before breakfast without leave and did not return till dinner time." The visitors Jane Inglis and Mary Bickle concluded that "as they seemed to have had no object in going away beyond that of taking a walk, the loss of their breakfast and a little admonition was deemed a sufficient punishment."[65]

The Committee of Management had various tactics at its disposal to encourage children's good behaviour. Corporal punishment is not mentioned explicitly in the HOA/LBS records until 1881, when rules governing its use were recorded, but it may have been applied prior to this.[66] The visitors' claim that certain boys did not "seem to feel" their punishment certainly suggests physical correction. Hasci claims that "corporal punishment was undoubtedly the most common method of dealing with disobedient children" in nineteenth-century American asylums.[67] In contrast, Janice Harvey found that the managers of Montreal's Ladies' Benevolent Society did not tolerate severe punishments. The Montreal Society dismissed a teacher in 1846 for "disciplining a boy with a strap."[68]

The Hamilton Orphan Asylum's visitors most frequently identified "confinement" of varying lengths of time as punishment for runaways and serious misbehaviour. The Committee of Management also seemed convinced that milder forms of discipline such as "a little admonition" would correct the behaviour of most children. These practices demonstrate an attempt to develop children's internal sense of conscience and self-government through persuasion rather than coercion. The most common forms of discipline meted out by the asylum's visitors were consistent with those of other childcare authorities who used corporal punishment sparingly. Houston and Prentice note that by mid-century Ontario schools began to use shame and deprivation instead of physical correction.[69] Mintz and Kellogg argue that after 1830 in the United States, "a growing number of experts believed that techniques designed to provoke guilt, such as confining children to their rooms, withholding love, or expressing parental disapproval, would be more effective in securing obedience than would physical punishment." Notably, women were assumed to best administer these forms of persuasion.[70]

The asylum that the Committee of Management and visitors envisioned bears little resemblance to its Dickensian counterpart. This institution was meant insofar as possible to provide children with a home, which the committee imagined in a very particular way. Whether children actually experienced this homelike atmosphere as such is impossible to know. These women were nonetheless empowered to normalize their particular conceptualizations of home and family and oversee its institutionalization within the asylum walls. This was a part of the orphan asylum's work over which the managers had considerable control. Although they had less control over the environment into which children were placed once they left the asylum, the committee's policies regarding adoption and apprenticeship also reveal these women's assumptions about proper familial relations.

Adoption

The Hamilton Orphan Asylum sometimes used adoption to place children out in families, even though it was a legal anachronism in this period.[71] This practice suggests that the Committee of Management could conceive of families as affective rather than merely hereditary units. These managers also demonstrated an understanding that the children they placed in private homes might be exploited for their labour and established policies during the mid-century to protect children from such abuse. The committee's adoption policies predate legal recognition of non-consanguineous families and may have protected more children from exploitation than other more prominent "child savers" of this era.

In the United States, Massachusetts established a statute in 1851 that became an archetype for adoption laws internationally.[72] The statute was based on a "child-centered model" in which prospective parents were required to demonstrate their "ability to bring up the child, and furnish suitable nurture and education."[73] Michael Grossberg has observed that the Massachusetts statute regarded children as "separate, if naturally dependent, individuals with their own needs and interests." This legal recognition of adoption "devalued natural ties" and redefined parental fitness by "standards of child welfare and nurture." In Grossberg's words, "artificial homes [were] permitted to supplant natural ones."[74]

In contrast, legal opposition to adoption in nineteenth-century England was strong. E. Wayne Carp attributes this opposition to "a desire to protect the property rights of blood relatives in cases of inheritance ... and the availability of other quasi-adoptive devices such as apprenticeship and voluntary transfers." He also notes that since children who were up for adoption were often of suspect parentage, the law avoided legitimizing a process that had the taint of immorality.[75] Adoption was not legally recognized in England until 1926.

In Ontario, the provincial government established no separate legislation governing adoption; nor was the legal status of adoption established until 1897. Legal conflict over adoption, such as inheritances, was left to the common law for resolution.[76] Nonetheless, the Hamilton Orphan Asylum's managers established specific policies regarding the transfer of children to adoptive parents and formalized written agreements to ensure that parents fulfilled the obligations of guardianship.[77]

According to the Committee of Management, any child admitted into the asylum under the age of five was eligible for adoption.[78] Apparently, this policy was sometimes overlooked. Neff found that nine boys and fourteen girls, whose names and ages were recorded in the Orphan's Register between 1848 and 1880, were adopted out. Six boys were under six years old and three boys were between six and eight. Ten of the girls were under six years, three were between six and eight, and one was older than eight. In other words, in about 30 percent of the orphan asylum's adoptions, children were over the age of five and thus not in accordance with the committee's own policy.[79]

Married couples who regularly attended a Protestant church were most likely to become guardians of the orphan asylum's children. Prospective parents were required to make an application to the Committee of Management, in which a couple might ask for a particular child they had chosen or, more commonly, simply identified whether a boy or a girl was preferred. A letter of recommendation from the prospective parents' minister was also required. If the minister's recommendation was good and the committee approved, a child would be sent out "on trial" for one month.

As an example, in March 1863, Mr. and Mrs. William Alland applied to adopt a little girl. The committee also received "a most satisfactory certificate" from their clergyman, Reverend James Black, and subsequently granted the couple's request.[80] This procedure apparently changed little over time. In December 1879, Mrs. Joseph Heron applied to adopt Jennie McAndrews and forwarded a letter from Reverend Leo Gaetz, who reported to the committee that Mr. and Mrs. Heron were "worthy of our trust and confidence."[81] Jennie was sent out on trial and eventually adopted by the Herons.

The Committee of Management often articulated an expectation that adoptive parents would raise the child as "their own." For example, in June 1862, two infants were found "lying on the Dundas road" and brought to the asylum by a Society member. According to the HOA/LBS's records, one of the children was "adopted by a respectable couple who have no children, to bring up as their own." The committee prepared "papers of adoption" for the couple to sign.[82] This expectation reveals managers' assumption that emotional bonds could overcome the lack of a hereditary link.

The Committee of Management clearly expected affective relations to develop between parents and adoptive children. When families failed to establish such an emotional bond, the committee willingly received adopted children back into the asylum. For instance, in September 1863, Mrs. Scott, who had adopted Lizzy Mangere in April, explained to the committee that "she could not excite any affection in the child" and therefore wished to return her to the asylum.[83] In another example from November 1867, Mrs. Campbell adopted three-year-old Isabella Quigley but sent her back to the asylum in December. The Committee of Management recorded that she "did not seem for some frivolous reasons to fancy the child."[84] These cases illustrate that the Committee of Management often received children back into the asylum when it was clear that the child and parents were not emotionally compatible, even if for seemingly "frivolous" reasons.

The Committee of Management also demonstrated some awareness that prospective parents might exploit an adoptive child. Although Neff has shown that the committee did not always abide by its own rules, it established a policy sometime before 1859 that stipulated that any child over the age of five was to remain in the asylum until age eleven.[85] This kind of policy seems to have been common in mid-century childcare institutions. Rooke and Schnell suggest that "all" orphan homes they studied "stipulated that older children, usually those over six or seven years, were not to be given out for 'adoption'" but legally placed in homes as apprentices.[86]

The case of Bertha Lewis illustrates the Committee of Management's policy's significance. Bertha was offered "a very desirable home" by a farmer in 1868. The committee, however, "objected to her *adoption* and preferred she should be bound out." The farmer was required to pay four dollars upfront and an annual payment of that amount until Bertha came of age. The money was deposited in a savings account "for her benefit."[87] In this way, the committee attempted to ensure that Bertha would not simply augment this family's pool of labour and that she would receive some recompense for her work. Apprenticeship was also a more secure form of agreement, as it was constituted in law. Without legal adoption statutes, an adoptee, such as Bertha Lewis, had no legitimate claim to an inheritance.[88]

This policy contrasts with the adoption practices of Maria Rye and Annie Macpherson, who were criticized by Andrew Doyle in his 1874 report to the British Department of Immigration. Rye and Macpherson placed thousands of immigrant pauper children from the United Kingdom with rural Canadian families between 1869 and 1875.[89] Rye, for example, allowed children to be adopted up to the age of nine. Children between nine and eighteen were indentured. This practice did not protect children who were younger than nine from exploitation as free labour and, according to Doyle's report, 90 percent of the children Rye adopted were placed "with a view to the future service of the child." A young girl's pithy remark to Doyle summed up the problem: "'doption, sir, is when folks gets a girl to work without wages."[90]

In 1881, the Committee of Management prepared and printed a set of rules for the Hamilton Orphan Asylum's management. It did not, however, indicate whether these were new rules or simply formalized versions of rules that had been in effect for some unspecified time. The rules regarding adoption were that "any person from partiality or love" who wanted to adopt a child of any age "into his own family ... as if it were his own child" could do so as long as all other rules regarding child placement were observed. For the Committee of Management, adoption remained a primarily affective rather than economic relationship. According to these rules, an adoptive parent was also required, as in apprenticeships, to pay a five-dollar fee to the Society, which was deposited in a savings account for the child's benefit to be paid out with interest when the child came of age. This policy allowed older children to be adopted out, but presumably payments were required to ensure that children would materially benefit from his or her placement since adopted children were not legally owed an inheritance.

The orphan asylum's adoption policies show, no less than its rules, that this institution's female managers wielded considerable influence over the lives of the children in their care. Their conceptualization of children as individuals with interests that ought to be protected and families as affective rather than simply hereditary units were instrumental to their decisions regarding adoptions. As the following section demonstrates, the Committee of Management's expectations for adopted children deviated from assumptions about children who were placed out of the asylum as apprentices.

Apprenticeship

Pauper apprenticeships, as mentioned in Chapter 3, were widely used by local governments and childcare institutions during the nineteenth century to cope with dependent children. The Hamilton Orphan Asylum was no exception, and its Act of Incorporation established the Committee of Management's legal rights and obligations regarding apprenticeship, which was discussed in Chapter 5.

The Committee of Management used a specific procedure that, like adoptions, changed little over time. Prospective masters or mistresses applied for either a particular child or any girl or boy the committee selected. Applications were accompanied by a recommendation from a minister and, if the Committee of Management deemed the situation suitable, a child would be sent on trial for one month. If the arrangement seemed satisfactory to all parties after the trial period expired, indenture papers would be signed, which committed masters or mistresses to provide their apprentice with food, clothing, shelter, an education, and religious instruction, as well as an annual fee for services rendered, which was held in trust for the child by the Society until his or her apprenticeship term expired. Only a few minor details were changed in the 1881 rules.

The committee's practices relative to apprenticed children differed significantly from those regarding adopted children. As discussed above, the committee willingly accepted adopted children back into the asylum whose caregivers failed to establish an emotional bond. In contrast, the managers only recorded re-admitting apprentices whose masters or mistresses were unsatisfied with their work. For example, Lily Lee was first taken on trial in July 1854 and returned five days later.[91] In November 1858, Lily was returned again to the asylum by another master who complained that "her extreme lazyness [sic] render[ed] her useless."[92] In June 1866, Harriet Cook was returned to the asylum "having been found entirely useless by her employers."[93] These practices demonstrate that apprenticeships were conceived as an economic relationship, the success of which was dependent upon a child's work ethic and performance.

Although the orphan asylum's policy dictated that children should not be apprenticed until age eleven, Neff found that on average 19 percent of boys and nearly 50 percent of girls apprenticed out of the asylum were under the age of nine.[94] Girls, who could perform various domestic chores from a young age, were often in high demand, whereas boys were probably taken to do heavier manual labour; therefore, masters usually requested older boys.

On the one hand, apprenticeship provided legal protection and a small wage for children and may have been preferable to adoption, until the provision of an allowance for adopted children was formalized in 1881. On the other hand, young children who were apprenticed out may very well have had their childhood cut short by masters and mistresses who treated them simply as servants. In 1881, however, the rules regarding apprenticeship raised the age of indenture to twelve for boys and fourteen for girls.[95] This adjustment suggests that during this period the appropriateness of apprenticing very young children had been called into question.

The committee expected both apprenticed and adopted children to be treated kindly, and managers made some effort to monitor the well-being of their former charges. Children sometimes voluntarily reported on their situations. In July 1863, the committee received "very satisfactory letters" from George Green and William Henderson, who reported they were "most happy in their new homes."[96] In September 1872, Lydia Jackson reported "five boys who were former inmates of the Asylum visited it during the Exhibition and all looked respectable and say they are doing very well."[97]

The neighbours and kin of children apprenticed from the asylum also sometimes volunteered news of ill treatment at the hands of guardians. The committee investigated reports of abused or neglected children, even in cases where the source of information was considered questionable.

For example, in March 1863, the committee reported a rumour concerning Robert Walsh, who had been apprenticed to Mr. Anderson. Although the managers recorded their opinion that the source of this rumour was "of doubtful authority," they dispatched Samuel Wilson to visit the child's master "with the ostensible reason of reminding [him] of two overdue annual installments." Wilson was directed to speak to the child alone and learn if the rumour was true.[98] Clearly, the committee was concerned not to accuse falsely Mr. Anderson on the basis of rumour. The possibility of abuse, however, was deemed important enough to warrant a personal investigation and a private interview with the child. Robert Walsh does not appear to have been re-admitted into the asylum, and, unfortunately, the outcome of Wilson's interview with the child was not recorded.

Although the committee received many complaints regarding the treatment of children placed out of the asylum and removed children willingly from abusive or neglectful homes, the managers did not devise alternative techniques to protect children. They continued to trust ministers' recommendations and rely upon sporadic reports from children, neighbours, and family, despite the obvious shortcomings and failures of this system. The problem did not go unrecognized, however. In 1868, at which time several reports of ill treatment had come to the attention of the committee, Harriet Juson recorded the query, "does it not seem as if we ought to devise of some more efficient means than we at present possess for looking after [the children who are placed out?]"[99] Nonetheless, the Committee of Management did not devise any such means at that time and continued in its former procedures. It was not until ten years later, in June 1878, that the committee resolved "that a corresponding secretary should be appointed, whose duty it should be to write periodically to the children who had left the Institution and so, in a measure, keep a watch over them."[100] The inadequacy of the orphan asylum's child placement procedures and its failure to protect children from abuse and neglect is a legacy shared among orphan asylums and child placement agencies of this – and other – eras.

The Committee of Management's policies and practices regarding children domiciled in the Hamilton Orphan Asylum and those apprenticed or adopted out demonstrate that, first and foremost, the principal goal was to provide homes for orphaned and dependent children. By and large, the committee assumed that these children could be trained "in the way that they should go" so long as a proper environment was provided for them. This environment, for the committee and visitors, necessarily included religious training, practical and academic education, and parental figures who provided structure and discipline, nurture and kindness, and opportunities for both work and recreation. Whether these expectations were met and if they met the needs of individual children are impossible to know. What is clear, however, is that the HOA/LBS's Act of Incorporation and financial support from local and provincial governments, as well as private donors, empowered the committee to devise rules, implement policies, and regulate the lives of children and their guardians as they saw fit.

7
Continuity and Change, 1870-93

At her death in 1875, at the age of seventy-one, Lydia Jackson was still actively serving as the HOA/LBS's treasurer, which was a position that she had held since 1853. In the intervening decades, her husband, Edward, had become one of the wealthiest men in Hamilton. Between the early 1850s and early 1870s, Hamilton transformed from "the ambitious little city" into "the Birmingham of Canada."[1] The Hamilton Tin Factory, which Edward founded in 1831, produced iron, tin, and copper products, as well as stoves and tinsmiths' equipment. During the 1840s and 1850s, numerous proprietors of small-scale shops in the metal trades, men such as Edward Jackson and his business partner Dennis Moore, as well as Edward Gurney, John Fisher, and Calvin McQuesten, became major economic players in Hamilton.[2]

Steel and iron manufacturing, which benefited from favourable tariff policies and substantial immigration into Canada's hinterlands, fuelled the city's industrialization during the 1870s.[3] The Great Western Railway, which was established in Hamilton in 1853, drove demand for metal products and became a major manufacturer and employer in its own right.[4] Textile mills and knitted goods manufacturing also flourished in the region.[5] Whereas about 24 percent of the workforce was employed in shops with ten or more employees in 1851, by 1871 this proportion was 83 percent.[6] Industrial capitalism had arrived in Hamilton.

The tumultuousness of rapid industrialization and class conflict shook the city and its social relations, as Bryan Palmer's analysis of 1870s Hamilton has shown. Although one might guess that the work of the city's most important private charity would have been dramatically altered by these changes, the HOA/LBS records show little evidence of major shifts in attitudes or practices. One of a few clues that the Society's work was affected was recorded in its 1872 annual report, which attributed the "limited number of children now in the institution" to "the great demand for the employment even of young children, in the workshops and factories of the city."[7] Indeed, in the early 1870s, one-third of Hamilton's workforce employed in the sewing-machine industry, for example, were children.[8] Circumstances in which young people could either fend for themselves or help their families by earning wages had a direct impact on demand for the Hamilton Orphan Asylum's childcare services.

The visiting society's work in outdoor relief was also affected by frequent boom-and-bust cycles, which were symptomatic of an unregulated industrial capitalist economy. During inflationary periods, the LBS noted that high costs of living exacerbated poverty in the city. In 1871, the annual report claimed that because "rents are now so high," donations were especially needed "to enable a poor widow or aged man to pay regularly for the roof which shelters them."[9] During times of economic downturn, such as the winter of 1874-75, the Society identified "scarcity of work" as cause for increased pressure on its charitable resources.[10] The 1878 report also captured the volatility of Hamilton's economy: "During the past winter, when so many were out of employment, your Society was called upon in several instances to give relief to those who in more prosperous times had given subscriptions to your Society."[11]

A change that affected the HOA/LBS's work at least as much as the economy was increased intervention by the provincial government into private and public forms of childcare and protection. The provincial government of Ontario passed a number of very significant pieces of legislation early in the 1870s. The first, passed in 1871, was compulsory education legislation, which empowered the state to legally charge parents who failed to send children between the ages of seven and twelve to school for at least four months per year.[12] This act was the province's first direct legal intervention into intact families that penalized parents directly for child negligence as defined by the state. The act also empowered public school boards to establish residential industrial schools, to which neglected children could be sent.[13]

A second piece of legislation, passed in 1874, provided a more detailed definition of industrial schools' roles within the public school system and indicated who might be sent to these institutions. An Act Respecting Industrial Schools allowed any person, including the child's parent, to bring a child under the age of fourteen to a magistrate, who was empowered to admit him or her to an industrial school until the age of sixteen. Children who were begging, homeless, destitute, orphaned, or "incorrigible" were candidates for industrial school admission.[14] Also, any child who "by reason of the neglect, drunkenness or other vices of parents, is suffered to be growing up without salutary parental control and education, or in circumstances exposing him to lead an idle and dissolute life" could be compelled into residence in one of these schools. This last condition was, as Charlotte Neff notes, the first time that Ontario legislation specifically "identified parental deficiencies as justifying societal intervention in the family."[15] The act also represented a clear legal paradigm shift from protecting parental custody rights to protecting the "best interest of the child."

Also in 1874, Ontario passed the Charity Aid Act, which, according to Richard Splane, "represented the first legislative attempt to express and enforce the province's right to require privately operated social welfare institutions ... to accept provincial inspection and to maintain standards deemed adequate for the performance of their functions."[16] In this explanation, Splane leaves the impression that theretofore private charities had operated outside of provincial legislation, which was not the case for childcare institutions with Acts of Incorporation. Also, prior to this point, charities like the HOA/LBS were not exempt from public inspection. The Act of Incorporation mandated that annual meetings were held that were open to the public and that full reports of the institution's affairs were sent to the provincial governor annually. Therefore, the 1874 act ought to be understood as transferring inspectoral power to state bureaucrats rather than imposing inspection ex nihilo.

The appointment of a civil servant to inspect charitable institutions was nonetheless highly consequential. J.W. Langmuir, a Scots Presbyterian who had worked in business and municipal politics, was appointed as an inspector, at the age of thirty-two, in 1868.[17] In 1874, he was appointed provincial inspector of asylums, prisons, and public charities under the auspices of the Charity Aid Act and granted extensive powers. He was authorized to compel charities to submit standardized registers of inmates' admissions and discharges, and he could revoke any institution's funding if its rules, regulations, and general management did not meet with his approval.[18]

Part of Langmuir's job was to create knowledge about welfare institutions in Ontario as a whole, thus his insistence on regularly kept registers, a rationalized funding formula, and systematic administration. The state's capacity to create and execute policy was dependent upon gathering standardized data related to local conditions. This work was disciplinary insofar as Langmuir's inspections created a corpus of knowledge about institutions that could facilitate their regulation. Bruce Curtis notes in his analysis of educational inspectors in Canada West, "inspection allowed the central authority to monitor the local operations of policy, to identify innovation and resistance, to form defensible conceptions of 'what needed to be done.'"[19] Thus, inspectors were the channel through which government policy affected and, to a lesser degree, was affected by local conditions.

One of Langmuir's first initiatives as inspector was bringing the attention of government to "certain defects and anomalies in the [funding] system."[20] These "defects" and "anomalies" were outcomes, at least in part, of granting decisions made based on the political capital of institutions' supporters rather than an assessment of individuals served or benefits accrued by charities' work. For example, Catholic institutions usually received smaller grants than Protestant ones, which Catholics argued was due to religious partisanship on the part of government. A rationalized granting system, which accorded institutions an equal, per inmate per day amount ultimately benefited Roman Catholic children's homes. Protestant homes and their supporters resisted the change.[21] In this case, standardization mitigated the effects of sectarianism in the provincial granting system. This and other techniques of government would not, however, eliminate Protestant bias in the system.

Curtis has pointed out that educational inspectors were "placed to promote and, at times, to enforce their cultural conceptions, their moral standards, their sense of justice, and their aesthetic sense as models for the rest of society."[22] In the context of nineteenth-century child welfare, these prerogatives had been granted to white, middle-class, Protestant women prior to provincial bureaucratization. Therefore, Langmuir's appointment can be seen as a shift of power from groups of women to one male civil servant. A key difference, of course, was that Langmuir was authorized to manage the power/knowledge nexus to much greater effect.

Langmuir, like many nineteenth-century inspectors, had no "expertise" per se and simply constructed knowledge and formed opinions about these institutions as he inspected them. His impressions were necessarily influenced, at least to some degree, by the policies and practices developed over many years by institutions' female managers. This was where managers' influence ended, however. Langmuir had the power to then define what was proper, orderly, and well-regulated or unacceptable, unsuitable, and inadequate. Once his judgments were adopted into policy, they obtained the gloss of expertise. This was the process by which white, middle-class, Protestant values became normalized within the provincial childcare regime and recognized simply as efficient, practical, and humane.

Apparently, the Hamilton Orphan Asylum's practices and policies were generally congruent with Langmuir's notions of a well-regulated institution. Langmuir inspected the asylum first in August of 1874 and, according to the Society's minutes, "expressed himself as highly pleased with the appearance of the children and the arrangement of the house and grounds."[23] In September 1875, the Committee of Management forwarded, at the inspector's request, a printed copy of the Society's bylaws, rules, and constitution.[24] When Langmuir inspected the asylum later that month, he was, apparently, "much pleased with Mr and Mrs Wilson's management" and declared that the institution was "in quite as good order as any ... he has visited."[25] The inspector continued to produce favourable reports about the asylum throughout the 1870s and early 1880s.[26]

Langmuir's inspections elicited a new level of intervention into the asylum's affairs by the HOA/LBS's trustees. The trustees' role had theretofore been, in their words, "mainly restricted to a formal expression of approbation."[27] In January 1876, however, the trustees attended the regular monthly meeting bearing a long list of recommendations that included alterations to the building, enlargement of the executive committee, an increase in membership fees, changes to the Society's bookkeeping system, and adjusting the time and frequency of committee meetings. Although the recommendations were left "for the Ladies to give their sanction," the secretary noted dryly that the trustees had "already appointed Mr. Dayfoot [a trustee] to see that the different works in the matter are properly done."[28]

The increased value of the HOA/LBS resources also stimulated a notable increase in male trustees' interest and involvement in the Society's affairs. In May 1875, the committee announced that, in a final act of charity, Lydia Jackson had bequeathed four thousand dollars to the Society in her will for the purpose of establishing a home for "aged and destitute women."[29] In April 1876, the HOA/LBS's finances were significantly enlarged once again by an endowment of seventeen thousand dollars from local philanthropist Albert Bigelow's estate. In June, for the first time in the Society's history, a male trustee, P.W. Dayfoot, chaired the regular monthly meeting. The significance was not simply symbolic. At this meeting, the committee voted their unanimous approval of the trustees' right to control the management of both Jackson's and Bigelow's legacies.[30]

While a great deal of consistency had marked the first twenty years of the Society's management, major changes in the personnel and size of the Committee of Management and visitors occurred during the late 1870s. By 1871, Hamilton's population had increased to 26,500, which was more than three times the city's size when the Society's sixteen visiting wards were first established. To cope with the city's population growth, in September 1874, the number of visiting society wards was increased to twenty-four, which required the services of forty-seven women. In 1876, the Committee of Management was also enlarged.[31]

Generational change also brought new members into the Society. Between 1875 and 1879, eight members of the committee, many of whom, like Lydia Jackson, were among the Society's founders, were replaced. More women also had a hand in the institution's management due to high rates of turnover. Whereas only forty-five women served on the Committee of Management between 1853 and 1875, ninety-four new members served on the committee from 1876 through 1879. These changes, however, were counteracted somewhat by familial ties: many "new" members were founders' and builders' daughters or daughters-in-law. For example, when Elizabeth Thomas, a founder, retired as president in 1876, her daughter Catherine Thomas Kerr, who had joined the association in 1851, took over her position.[32]

As of 1877, the HOA/LBS was also in charge of an entirely new branch of operations. Lydia Jackson's legacy led to a large addition to the orphan asylum building, which could accommodate twenty adult residents. The Committee of Management had hoped for some time to establish a custodial institution for several elderly women who had been dependent on the Society's outdoor relief for many years.[33] The Aged Women's Home, which was formally opened by the mayor in February, admitted women over sixty who had been residents of Hamilton for at least five years and were in good health.[34] As of September 1878, seventeen women had taken up residence in the home. The committee described their female clients as "not only unable in any way to provide for their own support but are friendless."[35] The records, however, do show that at least some of these women had adult children or other family.[36] For others, the only alternative to this institution was the House of Refuge.[37]

The establishment of a number of other childcare institutions in the city and province also changed the context in which the HOA worked. When the Hamilton Ladies' Benevolent Society first began taking in orphans, only one other specialized childcare institution existed in all of

FIGURE 1
Orphan Asylum (HOA) expenditures relative to population growth

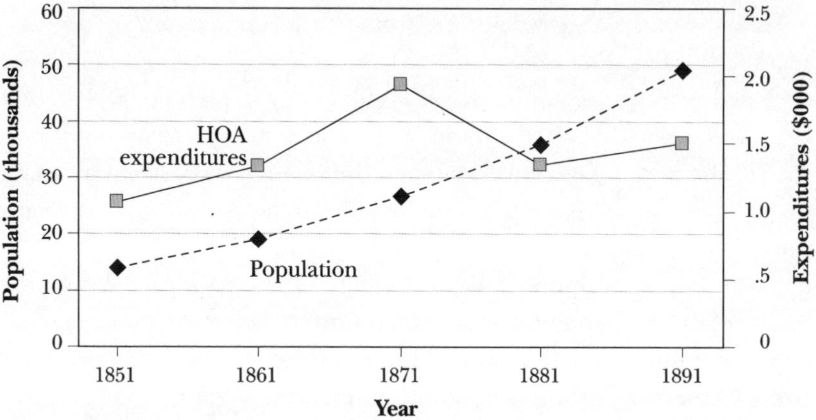

Source: Annual treasurer's reports provided the data for HOA expenditures. HAWHM, 1851-91, HPL. Expenditures for 1851 were converted from pounds sterling to dollars at a rate of 1 to 4.8666. "A History of the Canadian Dollar," www.bankofcanada.ca/wp-content/uploads/2010/07/1854-1914.pdf.

Canada West. By 1880, the Ontario government granted funds to eighteen institutions that provided residential care for over 1,300 children.[38] As of 1870, a Roman Catholic orphan asylum, as well as a Girls' Home and a Boys' Home, both of which cared for dependent children with parents, provided childcare services in Hamilton. The addition of these institutions was one of several factors, including demand for child labour and HOA managers' shifting priorities, that led to a general contraction in the HOA's services during the 1870s. Figure 1 illustrates that the extent of the HOA's work, as expressed in dollars spent, outstripped population growth throughout the 1850s and 1860s. In the following decade, expenditures declined sharply relative to the city's population and recovered only slightly in the 1880s.

Despite all of these changes, neither the HOA's practices nor its managers' rhetoric appear to have been substantively altered. When the Wilsons retired in 1879, after thirty-three years of service, they were replaced with two unmarried sisters. The committee, however, did not alter its expectations that the matrons would create a homelike atmosphere and provide kind and tender motherly care to both the children and aged women.[39] While the trustees played more prominent roles in the Society's legal and financial affairs,[40] the female managers continued to attend to the daily administration of the asylum, including decisions about admissions and discharges, and exercised both authorial and oratorical control over their annual reports.[41] The Orphan Asylum also continued to accept children with parents and willingly discharged them back to their families.[42]

Annual reports also varied little from the formula established in the 1850s and 1860s. The Committee of Management continued to provide evidence of its service to the public good. For example, the 1884 annual report recorded that after a fundraising concert in support of the visiting society, the mayor gave "an address on the value of this society, of which he had met many striking proofs in his visits to the poor families through the city."[43] Annual reports also continued to call attention to the positive impact of the association's childcare work. In the 1883 annual report, for instance, the corresponding secretary reported that of the nineteen children indentured from the asylum with whom she corresponded that year, "most of them are giving satisfaction, and all growing up into strong and useful men and women."[44] The Christian basis of the HOA/LBS's endeavours and rhetorical claims to God's approbation also remained consistent themes into the 1890s. In 1894, the annual report claimed that although the funds of the Society were very low, the committee "look forward confidently trusting our Heavenly Father, who giveth to all men liberally."[45] None of these reports evoked maternalism or the ideals of true womanhood to explain or justify the Society's work.

The committee and its supporters continued to worry about fraudulent claims upon the visiting society. In 1875, a letter, published in one of Hamilton's dailies and reprinted in the HOA/LBS's annual report, claimed that "[a] more thorough knowledge of parties soliciting relief would sometimes have saved the [LBS's] funds from imposition, or would have led to a more generous outlay." The committee defended itself by rearticulating its long-held commitment to the technique of visiting: "Your Committee would assure those who so generously subscribed to this charity that every care is taken, by personal inspection and enquiry on the part of the visitor, to guard against mistakes in either direction."[46]

Although the association's spending on outdoor relief had risen substantially through the 1850s and 1860s, by the 1880s its expenditures had dropped off and continued to decline in that decade (as illustrated in Figure 2). A general increase in the number of other charitable associations offering assistance to Hamilton's poor was likely a significant factor, which could have led to charitable donors directing funds elsewhere and/or a decline in applications. By the early 1880s, city directories listed seven

FIGURE 2

Outdoor relief (LBS) expenditures relative to population growth

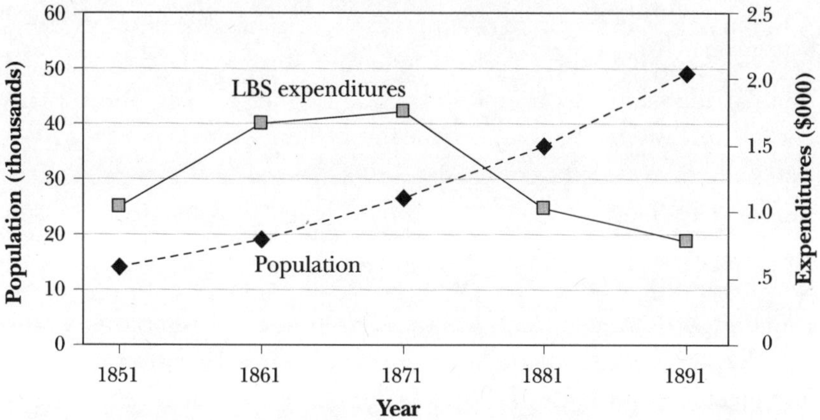

Source: Annual treasurer's reports provided the data for LBS expenditures. HAWHM, 1851-91, HPL. Expenditures for 1851 were converted from pounds sterling to dollars at a rate of 1 to 4.8666. "A History of the Canadian Dollar," www.bankofcanada.ca/wp-content/uploads/2010/07/1854-1914.pdf.

charitable institutions, not including those specifically for children, and seven benevolent societies.[47]

During the 1880s, the charity organization movement, which promised to improve charities' efficiency and effectiveness, was gaining popularity in the province.[48] At the forty-fifth annual meeting held on October 6, 1891, the HOA/LBS's president, Jane Stuart, put the Society at the forefront of local charitable innovation again by proposing that Hamilton's numerous charitable institutions unite. She suggested that this scheme, which "had proved useful in other cities," was the best means "whereby the danger of pauperizing our poor may be averted."[49] Adam Brown, one of the Society's trustees, offered to take the idea to the mayor, who subsequently called a meeting of benevolent societies to discuss the proposal.

By the end of November, Hamilton Associated Charities had been formed and received a $200 start-up grant from City Hall.[50] A Charity Savings Bank was also established as a "means of creating a spirit of thrift and consequent self help" amongst recipients of aid.[51] At the HOA/LBS's next annual meeting in 1892, the "liberal minded" and "philanthropic" were encouraged to "withhold their gifts" so that impostors were not encouraged in their "evil ways" and support the work of the Associated Charities instead so that appropriate "inquiries" could be made.[52] While this kind of rhetoric betrays harsh attitudes toward the poor, a central assumption that visitation was the most efficient form of providing outdoor relief, which was first espoused by the Society in 1846, was left unchallenged.

In 1894, the City began to take a much more active role in the distribution of charitable funds. Perhaps following Toronto's lead, which had done so one year prior, Hamilton's mayor assigned a relief officer.[53] This civil servant was to take charge of the books theretofore kept by the Associated Charities, which recorded the names of those receiving and requesting aid. The "ladies from the different Societies" were asked to "consult together, examine the Relief Officers [sic] Books, and make inquiries respecting the applicants."[54] In other words, direct responsibility for redistribution of charitable funds was transferred to a male employee of the City Corporation and the "ladies" were circumscribed to visiting the poor and making inquiries, so as to advise the officer about to whom relief should be given.

One year later, late in 1895, the City cancelled the annual grant that it had been forwarding to the HOA/LBS's visiting society since 1862, apparently because "the City Council had undertaken to do the work."[55] The president identified several reasons, in addition to the loss of the city grant, to justify suspending the visiting society's activities. She noted that the ward collections were not increasing equal to the demand for aid, that many other agencies in the city were involved in poor relief, and that the churches were providing more direct aid to the poor than in the past.[56] The Committee of Management and trustees held a special meeting about how to proceed. Although some agreed that LBS's work ought to be abandoned, others argued that it must continue since many deserving poor "would rather starve than apply to the city." In the end, the LBS decided to "continue their work but curtail the expenses one half."[57] The visiting society was eventually abandoned altogether in 1903.[58]

The most significant changes to the context in which the HOA/LBS worked, which ultimately led to the orphan asylum's demise, was a movement to replace childcare institutions with "foster homes."[59] During the early 1890s, private institutions such as the Hamilton Orphan Asylum began to sustain attacks from childcare "experts" and encounter general public disapprobation. E.A. Meredith, former chairman of the Board of Inspectors of Prisons, Asylums, and Public Charities, testified to Ontario's Prison Reform Commission in 1890 that fostering children was more effective and preferable to institutions.[60]

One of Canada's most prominent "child savers" was J.J. Kelso, who in 1887, as a twenty-two-year-old news reporter, successfully lobbied the provincial government for protective legislation for neglected children. He also spearheaded the establishment of a Children's Aid Society (CAS) in Toronto in 1891.[61] In 1888, due to Kelso's lobbying, Premier Oliver Mowat introduced An Act for the Protection and Reformation of Neglected Children. This legislation allowed judges to commit any child under fourteen who lacked proper guardianship, due to the "neglect, crime, drunkenness, or other vices of its parent ... or any other cause," either to an industrial school, as per the 1874 Industrial Schools Act, or a refuge or charitable institution.[62]

Although this act formalized certain public officials' authority to seize children on the grounds of parents' immorality and compel municipalities to pay for their maintenance, the Apprentice and Minor's Act of 1851 and any number of childcare institutions' Acts of Incorporation granted mayors and charitable institutions the legal power to abrogate the guardianship rights of any parent who did not or could not care for their children. In this context, the 1888 act represents a point on a continuum of state intervention into the private sphere of the family and not a radical departure from former laissez-faire state policy regarding children.[63]

Also due in large part to Kelso's lobbying, Ontario passed the Children's Aid Act in 1893, which granted Children's Aid Society officials wide powers to suspend parental rights and remove children from private homes that failed to meet government standards. The act also levied heavy penalties on parents or guardians convicted of mistreating or neglecting their children.[64] The power to fine parents up to one hundred dollars and/or imprison them for up to three months for their lack of good guardianship made this act substantively different from previous childcare legislation.[65]

In 1894, Kelso organized Ontario's first Conference on Child-Saving Work in Toronto. The HOA/LBS sent a delegation, including its president and financial and recording secretaries. The Committee of Management's report, however, was read out by one of the Society's trustees, Adam Hope Brown. The report appropriated child-savers' rhetoric regarding "fostering," implicitly arguing that the Hamilton Orphan Asylum's system of apprenticeship and adoption was indistinguishable from the CAS's putative innovation. The legal parameters of fostering bear striking similarity to indenture contracts, which similarly stipulated the provision of education, instruction in a "useful" occupation, "kind and proper treatment," and payment of a sum of money for the child at the age of majority.[66]

At the conference, according to the HOA/LBS's minutes, a proposal for "eventually absorbing all orphanages" into the CAS was made and apparently "vigorously combated both by Toronto and Hamilton representatives." In the end, the "issue was settled by an acknowledgement that the orphanages need not be interfered with ... as the Children's Aid Society's labour was directed to a different field."[67] In the years to come, the Hamilton Orphan Asylum nonetheless experienced a steep decline in demand for its services.

The Children's Aid Act ultimately marginalized private childcare institutions and made many of their services redundant. In 1893, the number of children in the Hamilton Orphan Asylum dropped from twenty to sixteen and, in 1894, the year Kelso established a CAS in Hamilton, from sixteen to thirteen.[68] By 1895, the committee, in an effort to fill available spaces in the asylum, announced that it would accept orphans from any place in Wentworth County.[69] By 1902, however, only four children were in the home.[70] The Hamilton Orphan Asylum ultimately closed its doors to children in 1915 after the government inspector, Dr. Helen McMurchy, informed the committee that it was unlawful to provide care to children and elderly persons in the same institution.[71]

Despite reformers' claims to radical improvement and innovation, the CAS tended to replicate rather than revolutionize nineteenth-century childcare practices.[72] For example, the CAS assigned voluntary visiting societies to watch over children placed in foster homes. This system appears to have been no more successful at protecting children than practices adopted by the Hamilton Orphan Asylum. Indeed, a representative from the Committee of Management at the 1894 Conference on Child-Saving Work explained that "in our work we have suffered from the want of a capable inspector to make regular visits and a thorough investigation of the homes in which our orphans are placed and apprenticed." The delegate suggested that the provincial government ought to appoint such an inspector, whose salary could be partially covered by the institutions themselves. The response from CAS representatives was that "the visiting Committees appointed by the various [CASs] ... could do all the work necessary."[73] Nonetheless, less than half the number of CAS volunteers required to adequately fulfill these duties were appointed and correspondence with foster parents was often the sole means by which committees were informed of children's well-being.[74]

The CAS also perpetuated Protestant biases within the system. Nancy Christie points to the importance of religion in framing family welfare policy prior to 1920 and the prevalence of anti-Catholicism in the CASs.[75] She asserts that "nowhere was the decidedly Protestant tenor of state welfare policies more clearly evident than in the implementation of the Child Protection Act. This legislation was unashamedly employed, both within government ranks and within the local children's aid societies, as a coercive tool for channeling recalcitrant Roman Catholic children into Protestant foster homes and thereby ensuring their rapid conversion."[76] Christie's observation that the ostensibly secular child welfare regime was very much informed by sectarian rivalries suggests that a great deal of continuity existed between voluntary childcare schemes in mid-century and those administered by the state later on.

During the last quarter of the nineteenth century, industrialization undeniably altered the conditions under which the HOA/LBS operated. Generational change, population growth, and increased involvement on the part of male trustees also contributed. These changes do not register as dramatically as those brought about by new levels of state involvement in charity and child welfare, however. Although the HOA/LBS's policies and practices changed remarkably little, the context in which it worked was very different by the end of the century. Regulation and inspection drew the Society and its work into the ambit of the state to a much greater degree than it had been before. While provincial legislation and the child-saving movement ultimately usurped charitable women's roles in nominally private institutions, ideologies and practices that were touted as innovations by late century "reformers" bore a striking resemblance to those that the HOA/LBS's Committees of Management and visitors had espoused since mid-century.

Conclusion
A Career in Christian Charity

The following obituary was penned by Nathanael Burwash and published in a local Hamilton newspaper shortly after Lydia Jackson's death:

> A valued citizen. Twenty-eight years ago at the foundation of the Ladies' Benevolent Society and Orphan Asylum of this City, she became more publicly connected with a career of Christian charity, which was uninterruptedly maintained to the day of her death. Great energy of character, and remarkable administration ability, guided by the soundest judgment, made her an acknowledged leader in all Christian work.[1]

Burwash's obituary suggests that charitable endeavours were a field of activity in which white, middle-class, Protestant women could become "publicly connected" with a "career" and lauded in public forums for their leadership skills and valuable work. Charitable women's activities were, in this case, those in which their administrative abilities, judgment, and energy of character were exercised successfully and appropriately. Burwash's rhetoric clearly designated philanthropic work as part of women's proper sphere. The case of the Hamilton Orphan Asylum and Ladies' Benevolent Society proves that women's charitable work and its implications ranged far beyond the domestic or strictly private. This obituary then begs the question: how do historians reconcile nineteenth-century separate spheres ideology, which insisted on middle-class women's relegation to the domestic sphere, with the general approbation that was accorded those who took on roles in charitable work?

The answer lies, in part, with political ideologies and discourses that sustained the private/public dichotomy in spite of the various ways that women's charitable endeavours challenged it. For most of the nineteenth century, legal disenfranchisement and restrictions on married women's property-holding gave state sanction to patriarchal ideology that rendered women non-citizens. The public sphere, as a discursively constituted political forum, consolidated women's political exclusion. Women's dependent status and their deviance from the ostensibly ideal, universal (male) political subject meant that women could not claim to speak on behalf of the public; nor could they represent themselves as "women in public."

When women are unable to represent their gender interests in legitimate forums, they cannot challenge their exclusion from politics or their unequal status in society. While acknowledging that "woman" is not a unitary category, mobilizing some sense of collective experience and identity is essential to any critique of systemic inequality based on gender. The discourses that constituted the public sphere rendered explicit articulation of gender interest de facto illegitimate and thereby prevented charitable women from formulating a political or empowering female identity.

A corollary to women's incapacity to self-represent has been men's prerogative to do it for them. This is perhaps most evident in the debates that took place in Hamilton in 1852 about city council's proposed building grant to the LBS. Public men on both sides of the debate wielded the discursive authority to represent charitable women's work in ways that served their own interests. Burwash's obituary and his longer eulogy of Lydia Jackson published in the *Canadian Methodist Magazine* are also iterations of this prerogative. In these texts, Burwash organized Jackson's life neatly within the confines of ideal Victorian womanhood. Her "great administration ability" was evident, first, in "the ordering of her domestic affairs" and, secondly, "in the management of various Christian enterprises." Jackson was also lauded for her "deepest domestic affections," "perfectly congenial and harmonious" marriage, and her "parental solicitude" toward her servants. For Burwash, she was "strong, earnest, active, and yet womanly."[2]

Burwash's capacity to transform Jackson into an idealized version of womanhood suitable for emulation demonstrates how men's authority over women's representation in public forums could have political effects. By situating her charitable work as one of several "Christian enterprises" and portraying Jackson as a paragon of domestic virtue, Burwash invoked religious and gender norms that restricted middle-class women to the private sphere. Even when women's lived experiences belied these restrictions, public men had the power to create a domesticated image and promulgate it amongst a general audience.

Gender historians and historians of women's voluntary associations who stress women's political agency can overlook or underestimate oppressive and powerful forces – of the discursive and political kind – that militated against women's empowerment. Certainly, a perspective that focuses entirely on oppression is hardly desirable, but one that ignores or fails to problematize those factors that did marginalize women is similarly undesirable.

Private Women and the Public Good has attempted to strike this fine balance. The opportunities that charitable work gave white, middle-class, Protestant women in Hamilton must be measured against the challenges of liberal and patriarchal discourses that constituted the public sphere. On the one hand, the Hamilton Orphan Asylum and Ladies' Benevolent Society's female managers and administrators were empowered to work on behalf of the public good, redistribute public and private monies, represent their work to the public gaze, influence public opinion, intervene in familial relations, and institutionalize their values and beliefs. On the other hand, this empowerment was constrained by men who wielded formal and informal authority to define, defend, criticize, and judge women's charitable work.

The preservation of charity as a private realm, despite its links to the state, served powerful interests. This case study shows that there were political benefits to maintaining a public/private dichotomy in the realm of social welfare. Private charity was a public good not only because it protected property owners' autonomy and limited state involvement in the economy. This arrangement also empowered the state to manage social welfare at arm's length and delegate its authority to particular interest groups. In Canada West, this assured the institutionalization of Protestant interests in charitable and child welfare provisions.

During the 1840s, the development of a political public sphere was concurrent with the implantation of a set of liberal values that formally and informally empowered white, Protestant, propertied men. In Hamilton, this latter group was small enough to identify. Men such as Edward Jackson, John Young, and Edward Cartwright Thomas accumulated capital, experience, and social connections that enabled them to take on leadership roles in local business, politics, and church and associational life. They belonged to a cohort for whom no part of public life was inaccessible and whose private interests came to be regarded as indistinguishable from the public good.

This cohort's prerogative to define the public good was derived, in part, by a political system that endowed property-owning men with local and provincial voting rights. It was also sustained by political ideologies and discourses that represented this group of men as more capable than others of bringing rational judgment to bear on issues of common concern and of speaking on behalf of the public. The female kin of white, Protestant, propertied men shared directly in neither of these prerogatives. They did, however, accrue derivative benefits that enabled them to take on the problem of poverty in Hamilton.

Religious, class, and gender norms that delegated charitable work to evangelical, middle-class women partially justified their endeavour. The LBS's appropriation of the techniques of scientific charity and organizational models of joint-stock companies also lent legitimacy. In order to succeed as a charity that relied on voluntary contributions, the LBS had to secure the favour of "the public." Female managers had at their disposal a rhetorical device, the annual report, which enabled them to make specific arguments about the efficacy of their charitable techniques and convince their audience that the association did indeed serve the public good. When the Committee of Management represented their work to the public, they defined it as a Christian duty. Invocations of Christian metaphors and images, like numerical evidence and rational management, had rhetorical power. Ultimately, it was as Christians rather than women that the HOA/LBS legitimized its work and on this basis secured public approbation and financial support.

The success of the LBS's early legitimizing project is evinced in a formal alliance with Hamilton City Council for the purpose of establishing an orphan asylum. The City had been intermittently directing public funds to the LBS since the council first convened in January 1847. The request for regular funding for an asylum, however, established a permanent private-public partnership. The City agreed to this request for several reasons, not least of which was the migration of thousands of Irish Roman Catholics into Hamilton, which had begun in 1847. The arrival of destitute and ill immigrants, many of whom had been made widows and orphans on their journey, created a crisis with which the City was ill-equipped to deal. Its partnership with the LBS helped the City attend to the problem of dependent children. This alliance shows that Hamilton's municipal government was willing to bear at least some financial responsibility for those who could not care for themselves and to use public monies to fund private charitable endeavours. The City's partnership also implicitly sanctioned the LBS's work and tacitly agreed that it served the public good.

The public debate that took place in 1852 over the LBS's request for additional funding from city council demonstrated clearly that the LBS's anomalous position – simultaneously a private institution and one that received public funding – created political tensions in need of resolution. The evangelical Protestant bias in the LBS's work alienated Roman Catholics, who countered the Society's claim that it served the public good. The liberal principle that protected liberty of conscience empowered Roman Catholics to challenge Protestant dominance over publicly funded social welfare institutions. In an effort to thwart Roman Catholic objections, the LBS's male supporters invoked discourses of women's "natural" benevolence and argued that the female managers were fundamentally "disinterested." These tactics attempted to designate the Society's work as private and thereby protect it from negative public scrutiny, as well as divert attention from the fact that the asylum did indeed serve particular religious interests at the expense of others. The City's decision to give the grant speaks to the success of these tactics. The LBS's decision to decline the grant shows the managers' unwillingness to accept the terms upon which it was granted – namely, that the mayor be granted a direct hand in the Society's management. Their written response, which, in contrast to their supporters' rhetoric, asserted that their work was in fact subject to the critical judgment of the public, suggests that the managers also rejected the grounds on which the grant had been justified.

Nonetheless, the LBS's male supporters' attempt to protect Protestant prerogatives over the care of dependent children was ultimately successful. Regular funding from city council continued to flow into the association's coffers. Members of the provincial legislature also collaborated by granting an Act of Incorporation to the association. This act transferred administrative and financial authority over the Hamilton Orphan Asylum and Ladies' Benevolent Society to a male board of trustees, while granting female managers wide discretionary powers over the lives of children who were entered into the asylum. Incorporation provided childcare institutions with state-sanctioned guardianship rights over children with or without parents. Therefore, the HOA/LBS was empowered to act either as a "protective" asylum that provided temporary care to children and willingly returned them to their parents or as an "isolating" asylum in which managers could insist that children be given up entirely to the institution. The extent and significance of powers delegated by provincial Acts of Incorporation to mid-century sectarian childcare institutions suggest that state-sanctioned interventions into intact families have a longer history than has been generally acknowledged.

The HOA/LBS managers' conceptualization of children as individuals with interests that ought to be protected and families as affective rather than simply hereditary units could be normalized within the institution and through their adoption and apprenticing practices. The Committee of Management assumed that the children in their care had needs that were fundamentally different from adults and that they were both innocent and susceptible to positive and negative environmental influence. Administrators also assumed that children had individual rights to fair, humane treatment, and that they would flourish in familial rather than institutional environments. A doctrine of "best interest," which posited that children were individuals with rights that superseded parental authority, enabled institutions such as the HOA/LBS to establish a standard of childcare and hold parents accountable to it, for better or for worse.

While other historians have argued that late nineteenth-century social reform projects, including childcare institutions, were manifestations of industrial capitalism and middle-class anxiety about social disorder, the HOA/LBS's work in the 1870s and 1880s continued very much as it had done for decades. Even increased state involvement in social welfare, through inspection and legislation, tended not to undermine the principles upon which the HOA/LBS were based. This latter development, however, did marginalize and ultimately supplant the association's role in both charitable provision and care of dependent children. The case of the HOA/LBS suggests that developments in the last quarter of the nineteenth century ought to be contextualized within a longer process of state formation, interference into families on behalf of children's best interest, and the institutionalization of Protestantism in social welfare.

In *The Structural Transformation of the Public Sphere,* Jürgen Habermas claims that the liberal, bourgeois public sphere that emerged in the post-Enlightenment West ultimately ceased to exist. Interestingly, he attributes its demise to the rise of social welfare states in the last quarter of the nineteenth century. As states began to play a larger role in private affairs, whether in economy or society, the boundary that divided private from public was permanently breached. Habermas observed that a "progressive 'societalization' of the state" and "increasing 'statefication' of society gradually destroyed the basis of the bourgeois public sphere – the separation of state and society."[3] Differentiation between private and public spheres no longer served the interests of states that sought to assert more control over private life or members of civil society who were willing – and sometimes eager – to facilitate these interventions.

The process by which states took on more responsibility for social welfare in the late nineteenth and early twentieth centuries, from Children's Aid Societies, to relief officers, to temperance legislation, was deeply interconnected with gender. New conceptualizations of "the social" that made healthcare, child welfare, sexual regulation, and domestic violence into public issues provided white, middle-class women with justifications for entry into these fields.[4] Indeed, these women were often at the forefront of pressure on the state to become more involved.[5]

In a classic article, Paula Baker claimed that when social policy became public policy, women's political fortunes also changed.[6] She tied state social welfare developments to politicization for women. Female suffrage, she argued, was "no longer either a radical demand or a challenge to separate spheres, because the concerns of politics and of the home were inextricable."[7] To put this into Habermasian terms, when the public (political) and the private (home) could no longer be sustained as dichotomous entities, the ideological basis of the public sphere was destroyed.

Women's gender interests could no longer be categorically excluded from political debate when women's issues were public issues. By the early twentieth century, women in the United States, Britain, and Canada evoked their special status as mothers and moral guardians to justify women's entry into professional social work, healthcare, law, and politics.[8] The efficacy of maternalist rhetoric in this particular historical moment suggests that the liberal, patriarchal public sphere had been radically reconstituted. How this shift in perspective might alter Canadian historians' understanding of the relationship among early twentieth-century politics, first-wave feminist rhetoric, and the social welfare state is an open question.

Notes

Introduction: Gender and the Public Sphere

1 Canadian historians have been more interested in nineteenth-century men's than women's associations. See Brian P. Clarke, *Piety and Nationalism: Lay Voluntary Associations and the Creation of an Irish-Catholic Community in Toronto, 1850-1895* (Montreal and Kingston: McGill-Queen's University Press, 1993); David A. Sutherland, "Voluntary Societies and the Process of Middle-Class Formation in Early Victorian Halifax, Nova Scotia," *Journal of the Canadian Historical Association* 5, 1 (1994): 237-63; Andrew C. Holman, *A Sense of Their Duty: Middle-Class Formation in Victorian Ontario Towns* (Montreal and Kingston: McGill-Queen's University Press, 2000); Jeffrey L. McNairn, *The Capacity to Judge: Public Opinion and Deliberative Democracy in Upper Canada, 1791-1854* (Toronto: University of Toronto Press, 2000); T.W. Acheson, "Evangelicals and Public Life in Southern New Brunswick, 1830-1880," in *Religion and Public Life in Canada: Historical and Comparative Perspectives,* ed. Marguerite Van Die (Toronto: University of Toronto Press, 2001), 50-68; Jean-Marie Fecteau and Éric Vaillancourt, "The Saint Vincent de Paul Society and the Catholic Charitable System in Quebec (1846-1921)," in *The Churches and Social Order in Nineteenth- and Twentieth-Century Canada,* ed. Michael Gauvreau and Ollivier Hubert (Montreal and Kingston: McGill-Queen's University Press, 2006), 195-224; Darren Ferry, *Uniting in Measures of Common Good: The Construction of Liberal Identities in Central Canada* (Montreal and Kingston: McGill-Queen's University Press, 2008); Michael Gauvreau, "Forging a New Space for Lay Male Piety: St. Vincent de Paul Societies in Urban Quebec and Ontario, 1846-1890," *Histoire Sociale/Social History* 42, 83 (2009): 35-67.

2 For a discussion, see Elizabeth Jane Errington, *Wives and Mothers, School Mistresses and Scullery Maids: Working Women in Upper Canada, 1790-1840* (Montreal and Kingston: McGill-Queen's University Press, 1995), 175-77.

3 For a discussion, see Richard B. Splane, *Social Welfare in Ontario, 1791-1893: A Study of Public Welfare Administration* (Toronto: University of Toronto Press, 1965); Rainer Baehre, "Paupers and Poor Relief in Upper Canada," in *Historical Essays on Upper Canada: New Perspectives,* ed. James Keith Johnson and Bruce G. Wilson (Ottawa: Carleton University Press, 1989), 305-40; Russell C. Smandych, "William Osgoode, John Graves Simcoe and the Exclusion of the English Poor Law from Upper Canada," in *Law, Society and the State: Essays in Modern Legal History,* ed. Louis Knafla and Susan W.S. Binnie (Toronto: University of Toronto Press, 1995), 99-128.

4 The Aged Women's Home's extensive records, held in the Hamilton Public Library, are an excellent source of information about elder care in Ontario from the late nineteenth through the twentieth century. The thematic and temporal scope of this institution is beyond that of this book. The AWH deserves its own historian.

5 Michelle Zimbalist Rosaldo, "Woman, Culture and Society: A Theoretical Overview," in *Woman, Culture and Society*, ed. Michelle Zimbalist Rosaldo and Louise Lamphere (Stanford, CA: Stanford University Press, 1974), 17-42. This notion has roots in Frederick Engels's argument that when industrialization moved productive work out of the home, the household "lost its public character" and women were relegated to "domestic slavery." Frederick Engels, *Origins of the Family, Private Property and the State*, ed. Eleanor Burke Leacock, original publication 1884 (New York: International Publishers, 1972).

6 In the United States, see Keith Melder, "Ladies Bountiful: Organized Women's Benevolence in Early 19th-century America," *New York History* 48, 3 (July 1967): 231-54; Carroll Smith-Rosenberg, *Religion and the Rise of the American City: The New York City Mission Movement, 1812-1870* (Ithaca, NY: Cornell University Press, 1971); Nancy Cott, *The Bonds of Womanhood: Woman's Sphere in New England, 1780-1835* (New Haven, CT: Yale University Press, 1977); Barbara Berg, *The Remembered Gate: Origins of American Feminism, the Woman and the City, 1800-1860* (New York: Oxford University Press, 1978). In Canada, see Wendy Mitchinson, "The WCTU: 'For God, Home and Native Land': A Study in Nineteenth-Century Feminism," in *A Not Unreasonable Claim: Women and Reform in Canada, 1880s-1920s*, ed. Linda Kealey (Toronto: Women's Press, 1979), 151-67; and Sharon Anne Cook, *Through Sunshine and Shadow: The Woman's Christian Temperance Union, Evangelicalism, and Reform in Ontario, 1874-1930* (Montreal and Kingston: McGill-Queen's University Press, 1995).

7 The US literature includes Mary P. Ryan, *The Cradle of the Middle Class: The Family in Oneida County, New York, 1790-1865* (Cambridge: Cambridge University Press, 1981); Nancy Hewitt, *Women's Activism and Social Change, Rochester, New York, 1822-1872* (Ithaca, NY: Cornell University Press, 1984); Lori D. Ginzberg, *Women and the Work of Benevolence: Morality, Politics, and Class in the Nineteenth-Century United States* (New Haven, CT: Yale University Press, 1990). In Britain, see Leonore Davidoff and Catherine Hall, *Family Fortunes: Men and Women of the English Middle Class, 1780-1850* (Chicago: University of Chicago Press, 1987) and F.K. Prochaska, *Women and Philanthropy in Nineteenth-Century England* (Oxford: Clarendon Press, 1980). In Canada, see Mariana Valverde, *The Age of Light, Soap and Water: Moral Reform in English Canada, 1885-1925* (Toronto: McClelland and Stewart, 1991).

8 See especially Linda K. Kerber, "Separate Spheres, Female Worlds, Woman's Place: The Rhetoric of Women's History," *Journal of American History* 75, 1 (1988): 9-39.

9 In the United States, see as examples Kerber, "Separate Spheres"; Mary P. Ryan, *Women in Public: Between Banners and Ballots, 1825-1880* (Baltimore, MD: Johns Hopkins University Press, 1990); Kathleen D. McCarthy, ed., *Lady Bountiful Revisited: Women, Philanthropy and Power* (New Brunswick: Rutgers University Press, 1990); Anne Firor Scott, *Natural Allies: Women's Associations in American History* (Urbana: University of Illinois Press, 1991); Carolyn J. Lawes, *Women and Reform in a New England Community, 1815-1860* (Lexington: University Press of Kentucky, 2000); Anne M. Boylan, *The Origins of Women's Activism: New York and Boston, 1797-1840* (Chapel Hill: University of North Carolina Press, 2002); Kathleen McCarthy, *American Creed: Philanthropy and the Rise of Civil Society, 1700-1865* (Chicago: University of Chicago Press, 2003). In Britain, see Maria Luddy, *Women and Philanthropy in Nineteenth-Century Ireland* (Cambridge: Cambridge University Press, 1995); Eleanor Gordon and Gwyneth Nair, *Public Lives: Women, Family and Society in Victorian Britain* (New Haven, CT: Yale University Press, 2003). In Canada, see Marguerite Van Die, "Revisiting 'Separate Spheres': Women,

Religion, and the Family in Mid-Victorian Brantford, Ontario," in *Households of Faith: Family, Gender and Community in Canada, 1760-1969*, ed. Nancy Christie (Montreal and Kingston: McGill-Queen's University Press, 2001), 234-63; and Janice Harvey, "The Protestant Orphan Asylum and the Montreal Ladies' Benevolent Society: A Case Study in Protestant Child Charity in Montreal, 1822-1900," (PhD diss., McGill University, 2001).

10 Rosaldo made this observation in her response to the uses and, in her words, abuses of the arguments she made in her 1974 article. Michelle Zimbalist Rosaldo, "The Use and Abuse of Anthropology: Reflections on Feminism and Cross-Cultural Understanding," *Signs* 5, 3 (1980): 389-417. Linda Kerber also makes this point, which she, paradoxically, contradicts in her discussion of space and women's subordination. Kerber, "Separate Spheres," esp. 31-32, 38.

11 See Nancy Fraser, "What's Critical about Critical Theory? The Case of Habermas and Gender," *New German Critique* 35 (Spring/Summer 1985): 97-131 and "Rethinking the Public Sphere: A Contribution to the Critique of Actually Existing Democracy," in *Habermas and the Public Sphere*, ed. Craig Calhoun (Cambridge, MA: MIT Press, 1992), 110-34; Carole Pateman, "Feminist Critiques of the Public/Private Dichotomy," in *Feminism and Equality*, ed. Anne Phillips (New York: New York University Press, 1987), 103-26; Joan B. Landes, *Women and the Public Sphere in the Age of French Revolution* (Ithaca, NY: Cornell University Press, 1988); Johanna Meehan, ed., *Feminists Read Habermas: Gendering the Subject of Discourse* (New York: Routledge, 1995); Seyla Benhabib, "Models of Public Space: Hannah Arendt, the Liberal Tradition, and Jurgen Habermas," in *Feminism, the Public and the Private*, ed. Joan B. Landes (Oxford: Oxford University Press, 1998), 65-99.

12 See Mary P. Ryan, "Gender and Public Access: Women's Politics in Nineteenth-Century America," in *Habermas and the Public Sphere*, ed. Craig Calhoun (Cambridge, MA: MIT Press, 1992), 259-88. For critiques, see Harold Mah, "Phantasies of the Public Sphere: Rethinking the Habermas of Historians," *Journal of Modern History* 72 (March 2000): 153-82; and Carmen Nielson Varty, "'A Career in Christian Charity': Women's Benevolence and the Public Sphere in a Mid-Nineteenth-Century Canadian City," *Women's History Review* 14, 2 (2005): 243-64.

13 Jürgen Habermas, *The Structural Transformation of the Public Sphere: An Inquiry into the Category of Bourgeois Society*, 1962, translated by Thomas Burger with assistance from Frederick Lawrence (Cambridge, MA: MIT Press, 1989), 83-85.

14 Ibid., 28.

15 Ibid., 54-55.

16 Mah, "Phantasies of the Public Sphere," 167.

17 Ibid., 155.

18 Ibid., 166.

19 For discussions, see Carole Pateman, *The Sexual Contract: Aspects of Patriarchal Liberalism* (Stanford, CA: Stanford University Press, 1988); Landes, *Women and the Public Sphere;* Joan Wallach Scott, *Gender and the Politics of History* (New York: Columbia University Press, 1988).

20 Habermas, *The Structural Transformation of the Public Sphere*, 85.

21 Ibid., 87.

22 Ibid.

23 For a discussion, see Hannah Arendt, *The Human Condition*, 2nd ed. (Chicago: University of Chicago Press, 1998).

24 Lori Chambers, *Married Women and Property Law in Victorian Ontario* (Toronto: University of Toronto Press, 1997) and Constance Backhouse, "Married Women's Property Law in Nineteenth-Century Canada," *Law and History Review* 6, 2 (1988): 211-57.

25 Bettina Bradbury, "Women at the Hustings: Gender, Citizenship, and the Montreal By-Elections of 1832," in *Rethinking Canada: The Promise of Women's History*, 5th ed., ed. Mona Gleason and Adele Perry (Toronto: Oxford University Press Canada, 2006), 73-94.

26 Ian McKay, "The Liberal Order Framework: A Prospectus for a Reconnaissance of Canadian History," *Canadian Historical Review* 81, 4 (2000): 617-45. For further elaboration, see Ian McKay, "Canada as a Long Liberal Revolution: On Writing the History of Actually Existing Canadian Liberalisms, 1840s-1940s," in *Liberalism and Hegemony: Debating the Liberal Revolution*, ed. Jean-François Constant and Michel Ducharme (Toronto: University of Toronto Press, 2009), 347-452.

27 McKay, "The Liberal Order Framework," 623.

28 See Constant and Ducharme, *Liberalism and Hegemony* for debates on these principles and their relative importance in liberal theory.

29 For relevant discussions, see Philip Corrigan and Derek Sayer, eds., *The Great Arch: English State Formation as Cultural Revolution* (Oxford: Basil Blackwell, 1985); Bruce Curtis, *True Government by Choice Men? Inspection, Education, and State Formation in Canada West* (Toronto: University of Toronto Press, 1992); Allan Greer and Ian Radforth, eds., *Colonial Leviathan: State Formation in Mid-Nineteenth-Century Canada* (Toronto: University of Toronto Press, 1992), especially Lykke De la Cour, Cecilia Morgan and Mariana Valverde, "Gender Regulation and State Formation in Nineteenth-Century Canada," 163-91 and Jean-Marie Fecteau, "État et associationnisme as XIXe siècle québécois: elements pour une problématique des rapports État/société dans la transition au capitalism," 134-62; and J.I. Little, *State and Society in Transition: The Politics of Institutional Reform in the Eastern Townships, 1838-1852* (Montreal and Kingston: McGill-Queen's University Press, 1997).

30 Mariana Valverde, "The Mixed Social Economy as Canadian Tradition," *Studies in Political Economy* 47 (Summer 1995): 33-59.

31 James Kaufman, "Corporate Law and the Sovereignty of States," *American Sociological Review* 73 (June 2008): 402-3.

32 The broad contours of modern childhood have been set out by two seminal works: Phillip Ariès, *Centuries of Childhood: A Social History of Family Life* (New York: Knopf, 1962) and Viviana A. Rotman Zelizer, *Pricing the Priceless Child: The Changing Social Value of Children* (New York: Basic Books, 1985). Influential older studies that did identify late-century interventions as radical innovations include Splane, *Social Welfare in Ontario;* Neil Sutherland, *Children in English-Canadian Society: Framing the Twentieth-Century Consensus* (Toronto: University of Toronto Press, 1976); and Andrew Jones and Leonard Rutman, *In the Children's Aid: J.J. Kelso and Child Welfare in Ontario* (Toronto: University of Toronto Press, 1981).

33 Patricia T. Rooke and R.L. Schnell, *Discarding the Asylum: From Child Rescue to the Welfare State in English Canada (1800-1950)* (Lanham, MD: University Press of America, 1983); John Bullen, "J.J. Kelso and the 'New' Child-Savers: The Genesis of the Children's Aid Movement in Ontario," *Ontario History* 82, 2 (1990): 107-28; Veronica Strong-Boag, *Finding Families, Finding Ourselves: English Canada Encounters Adoption from the Nineteenth Century to the 1990s* (Don Mills, ON: Oxford University Press, 2006); Charlotte Neff, "The Role of Protestant Children's Homes in Nineteenth-Century Ontario: Child Rescue or Family Support?" *Journal of Family History* 34, 1 (2009): 48-88; Veronica

Strong-Boag, *Fostering Nation? Canada Confronts Its History of Childhood Disadvantage* (Waterloo, ON: Wilfrid Laurier University Press, 2011).

Chapter 1: Hamilton, Upper Canada to 1846

1 Hamilton's rich historical record provides a solid base upon which to build this study. Academic monographs include: Michael Katz, *The People of Hamilton, Canada West: Family and Class in a Mid-Nineteenth-Century City* (Cambridge, MA: Harvard University Press, 1975); Bryan D. Palmer, *A Culture in Conflict: Skilled Workers and Industrial Capitalism in Hamilton, Ontario, 1860-1914* (Montreal and Kingston: McGill-Queen's University Press, 1979); John C. Weaver, *Hamilton: An Illustrated History* (Toronto: James Lorimer and Company, 1982) and *Crimes, Constables, and Courts: Order and Transgression in a Canadian City, 1816-1970* (Montreal and Kingston: McGill-Queen's University Press, 1995); Robert Kristofferson, *Craft Capitalism: Craftworkers and Early Industrialization in Hamilton, 1840-1870* (Toronto: University of Toronto Press, 2007).

2 Nathanael Burwash, "Edward and Lydia Ann Jackson," part I, *Canadian Methodist Magazine, Devoted to Religion, Literature, and Social Progress* 3, 1 (January 1876): 2-3.

3 Burwash, "Edward and Lydia Ann Jackson," part I, 4.

4 Weaver, *Hamilton,* 15-16.

5 Douglas McCalla, *Planting the Province: The Economic History of Upper Canada 1784-1870* (Toronto: University of Toronto Press, 1993).

6 Burwash, "Edward and Lydia Ann Jackson," part I, 4.

7 Bruce Curtis, "Social Investment in Medical Forms: The 1866 Cholera Scare and Beyond," *Canadian Historical Review* 81, 3 (2000): 347-79.

8 G.J. Parr, "The Welcome and the Wake, Attitudes in Canada West toward the Irish Famine Migration," *Ontario History* 66, 2 (1974): 101-13.

9 Burwash, "Edward and Lydia Ann Jackson," part I, 5.

10 Michael Gauvreau, "Protestantism Transformed: Personal Piety and the Evangelical Social Vision, 1815-1867," in *The Canadian Protestant Experience 1760-1990,* ed. George A. Rawlyk (Montreal and Kingston: McGill-Queen's University Press, 1990), 61-63.

11 Burwash, "Edward and Lydia Ann Jackson," part I, 7.

12 Marjorie Campbell, *A Mountain and a City: The Story of Hamilton* (Toronto: McClelland and Stewart, 1996), 70.

13 Weaver, *Hamilton,* 38-39.

14 Quoted in Michael Doucet and John C. Weaver, "Town Fathers and Urban Continuity: The Roots of Community Power and Physical Form in Hamilton, Upper Canada, in the 1830s," in *Historical Essays on Upper Canada: New Perspectives,* ed. J.K. Johnson and Bruce G. Wilson (Ottawa: Carleton University Press, 1989), 435-36.

15 Campbell, *A Mountain and a City,* 62.

16 Weaver, *Crimes, Constables, and Courts,* 48.

17 Curtis, *True Government,* 19.

18 *Western Mercury (Hamilton),* April 24, 1834, 2.

19 Splane, *Social Welfare in Ontario,* 65-73.

20 Board of Police meeting minutes, September 1840-April 1846, Hamilton City Council Minutes (HCCM), microfilm 105, vol. 1, 204, 206, 303-4, 308; vol. 2, 4, 78, Hamilton Public Library Local History and Archives Department (HPL).

21 For a discussion of this process and its economic and cultural implications, see Winifred Rothenberg, *From Market Places to a Market Economy: The Transformation of Rural Massachusetts, 1750-1850* (Chicago: University of Chicago Press, 1992).

22 For a discussion of the importance of merchants to local credit systems in Upper Canada, see McCalla, *Planting the Province.*
23 See, for example, *Hamilton Spectator,* July 21, 1847; and Weaver, *Hamilton,* 56.
24 See, for example, *Gore Gazette,* June 9, 1827, 4; *Dundas Weekly Post,* November 21, 1834, 3.
25 Curtis, *True Government,* 200n16.
26 Ibid., 16.
27 Ibid., 6-7, 10.
28 McNairn, *The Capacity to Judge,* 63.
29 Ibid., 68.
30 Ibid., 69.
31 Ibid.
32 Ibid., 118-22.
33 Thomas Melville Bailey et al., eds., *Dictionary of Hamilton Biography* 1, s.v. "Edward Cartwright Thomas," 194.
34 Ibid., s.v. "George Perkins Boothesby Bull," 37.
35 Campbell, *A Mountain and a City,* 98-99.
36 Doucet and Weaver, "Town Fathers and Urban Continuity," 427.
37 Ibid., 440.
38 Weaver, *Hamilton,* 12.
39 Ibid., 27.
40 Act to alter and amend the Act incorporating the Town of Hamilton, and to erect the same into a City, Statutes of the Province of Canada, ch. 73 (1846), 981-1005.
41 *Hamilton Spectator,* October 1846, qtd. in Brian Henley, *1846 Hamilton: From a Frontier Town to the Ambitious City* (Hamilton: North Short Publishing, 1995), 84-85.
42 *Hamilton Spectator,* December 1846, qtd. in ibid., 85.
43 *Hamilton Spectator,* January 1847, qtd. in ibid., 90.
44 Ibid., 91.
45 Bailey et al., eds., *Dictionary of Hamilton Biography,* s.v. "Colin Campbell Ferrie," by John C. Weaver, 74-75.
46 Ibid., s.v. "John Willson," by Robert L. Fraser, 212-14.
47 Katz, *People of Hamilton,* 178-87.
48 Ibid., 184, 186, 187.
49 Hamilton Aged Women's Home Minutes (HAWHM), various dates, HPL; Bailey et al., eds., *Dictionary of Hamilton Biography.*
50 Haley P. Bamman, "The Ladies Benevolent Society of Hamilton, Ontario: Form and Function in Mid-Nineteenth Century Urban Philanthropy," in *The Canadian Social History Project, Interim Report No. 4,* ed. Michael B. Katz (Toronto: Department of History and Philosophy of Education, Ontario Institute for Studies in Education, 1972), 182.
51 Bailey et al., eds., *Dictionary of Hamilton Biography,* s.v. "Edward Cartwright Thomas," 194.
52 Ibid., s.v. "Hugh Cossart Baker," 12-13.
53 Ibid., s.v. "John Young," 217.
54 Ibid., s.v. "Alexander Gale," 78-79.
55 Ibid., s.v. "William Patterson McLaren," 134.
56 Ibid.
57 Ibid., s.v. "Richard Juson," 111-12.
58 Katherine Greenfield, "The Reverend John Gamble Geddes and Early Days at Christ's Church Hamilton," *Wentworth Bygones* 4 (1963): 17.

59 Bailey et al., eds., *Dictionary of Hamilton Biography,* s.v. "Edward Jackson," 108-9; Nathanael Burwash, "Edward and Lydia Ann Jackson," part II, *Canadian Methodist Magazine, Devoted to Religion, Literature, and Social Progress* 3, 2 (February 1876): 98-99.

Chapter 2: A "sufficiently extensive and efficient instrumentality"

1 HAWHM, May 20, 1846, HPL.

2 David Owen, *English Philanthropy, 1660-1960* (Cambridge, MA: Harvard University Press, 1964).

3 Eileen Janes Yeo, *The Contest for Social Science: Relations and Representations of Gender and Class* (London: Rivers Oram Press, 1996), 24.

4 For discussions see Ryan, *Cradle of the Middle Class;* Davidoff and Hall, *Family Fortunes;* and Holman, *A Sense of Their Duty.*

5 Hugh Cunningham, Introduction to *Charity, Philanthropy and Reform from the 1690s to 1850,* ed. Hugh Cunningham and Joanna Innes (London: Macmillan Press, 1998), 4. See also Jeroen J. H. Dekker, "Transforming the Nation and the Child: Philanthropy in the Netherlands, Belgium, France and England, c. 1780-c. 1850," in ibid., 130-47.

6 John Webster Grant, *A Profusion of Spires: Religion in Nineteenth-Century Ontario* (Toronto: University of Toronto Press, 1988), 105, 167.

7 Smith-Rosenberg, *Religion and the Rise of the American City,* 3-4.

8 Gauvreau, "Protestantism Transformed," 61. See also Marguerite Van Die, *An Evangelical Mind: Nathanael Burwash and the Methodist Tradition in Canada, 1839-1918* (Montreal and Kingston: McGill-Queen's University Press, 1989), 10.

9 Cott, *The Bonds of Womanhood;* Smith-Rosenberg, *Religion and the Rise of the American City;* Hewitt, *Women's Activism and Social Change;* Ryan, *Cradle of the Middle Class;* Davidoff and Hall, *Family Fortunes;* Ginzberg, *Women and the Work of Benevolence;* Van Die, "Revisiting 'Separate Spheres.'"

10 Two Roman Catholic women, Mary Stuart MacNab, who was the wife of prominent Hamilton politician Allan MacNab, and Mary Egan, the president of the St. Mary's Benevolent Society, were honorary members in 1846 and 1850, respectively.

11 HAWHM, May 5, 1847; June 14, 1848; June 12, 1850, HPL. The treasurer's report for 1849 is not included in the LBS's records.

12 Alan Kidd, *State, Society, and the Poor in Nineteenth-Century England* (New York: St. Martin's Press, 1999); Yeo, *The Contest for Social Science;* and Donna T. Andrew, *Philanthropy and Police: London Charity in the Eighteenth Century* (Princeton, NJ: Princeton University Press, 1989).

13 Yeo, *The Contest for Social Science,* 4-5.

14 Michael J.D. Roberts, "Head versus Heart? Voluntary Associations and Charity Organization in England, c. 1700-1850," in *Charity, Philanthropy and Reform,* 70; Owen, *English Philanthropy,* 98.

15 Yeo, *Contest for Social Science,* 5; Roberts, "Head versus Heart?" 70; Owen, *English Philanthropy,* 98.

16 Thomas Robert Malthus, *An Essay on the Principle of Population,* 531, qtd. in Roberts, "Head versus Heart?" 74.

17 Yeo, *The Contest for Social Science,* 6, 67.

18 See discussions in Anne Summers, "A Home from Home – Women's Philanthropic Work in the Nineteenth Century," in *Fit Work for Women,* ed. Sandra Burman (New York: St. Martin's Press, 1979), 33-63; Ginzberg, *Women and the Work of Benevolence;* Smith-Rosenberg, *Religion and the Rise of the American City;* Christine Stansell, *City of*

Women: Sex and Class in New York, 1789-1860 (New York: Knopf, 1982); and Hewitt, *Women's Activism and Social Change.*

19 Scott, *Natural Allies;* Yeo, *The Contest for Social Science;* Ryan, *Women in Public.*

20 Yeo, *The Contest for Social Science,* 15.

21 Cunningham, Introduction to *Charity, Philanthropy and Reform,* 6; Prochaska, *Women and Philanthropy,* 98.

22 For descriptions of visiting societies' modes of organization, see Owen, *English Philanthropy,* 12; Prochaska, *Women and Philanthropy,* 105; Holman, *A Sense of Their Duty,* 111-12; Scott, *Natural Allies,* 13.

23 HAWHM, May 20, 1846, HPL.

24 Ibid., June 28, 1848.

25 Ibid., May 20, 1846.

26 Ibid., November 30, 1846; February 22, 1847; April 26, 1847; May 5, 1847.

27 Ibid., May 5, 1847.

28 Robert White and Dallas Hanson, "Rationality and Rhetoric in the Corporate World: The Corporate Annual Report as an Aristotelian Genre," *Prometheus* 18, 3 (2000): 303-17.

29 HAWHM, May 5, 1847, HPL.

30 Ibid.

31 Ibid., May 5, 1847; June 14, 1848; June 8, 1849; June 12, 1850; July 15, 1851; October 19, 1859; October 29, 1862; November 16, 1864; November 1, 1865; October 23, 1867; November 12, 1870; November 8, 1871; November 6, 1872; November 5, 1873; September 30, 1874.

32 Ibid., May 5, 1847.

33 Ibid., June 12, 1850.

34 Ibid., May 5, 1847; June 8, 1849; June 14, 1848; June 8, 1849; June 12, 1850; October 29, 1862; October 28, 1863.

35 Ibid., May 5, 1847; June 14, 1848; June 8, 1849; July 15, 1851; June 15, 1852; February 6, 1854; April 9, 1855; February 5, 1857; February 3, 1858; October 19, 1859; January 2, 1861; November 1, 1865; October 23, 1867; November 12, 1870; November 8, 1871; November 5, 1873; September 30, 1874.

36 Cunningham, Introduction to *Charity, Philanthropy and Reform,* 3.

37 HAWHM, June 14, 1848, HPL.

38 Ibid., February 6, 1854.

39 Ibid., October 28, 1863.

40 Ibid., February 3, 1858.

41 Sandra Sherman, *Imagining Poverty: Quantification and the Decline of Paternalism* (Columbus: Ohio State University Press, 2001), 3.

42 Ibid., 4-5.

43 Joan Wallach Scott makes similar observations in her discussion of statistics and the discourse of social reform in early nineteenth-century France. See Scott, *Gender and the Politics of History,* 113-15. For another pertinent discussion, see Bruce Curtis, *The Politics of Population: State Formation, Statistics, and the Census of Canada, 1840-1875* (Toronto: University of Toronto Press, 2001).

44 See Michael Gauvreau, *The Evangelical Century: College and Creed in English Canada from the Great Revival to the Great Depression* (Montreal and Kingston: McGill-Queen's University Press, 1991), especially Chapters 1 and 2.

45 HAWHM, July 15, 1851, HPL.

46 Ibid., February 5, 1857.

47 Ibid., February 6, 1854.

48 Ibid., October 28, 1863.

49 For discussions of women's use of religious metaphors to justify non-domestic activities, see Susan Zaeske, *Signatures of Citizenship: Petitioning, Antislavery, and Women's Political Identity* (Chapel Hill: University of North Carolina Press, 2003), esp. 59-60; Eileen Janes Yeo, ed., *Radical Femininity: Women's Self-representation in the Public Sphere* (Manchester: Manchester University Press, 1998); Van Die, "Revisiting 'Separate Spheres.'"

50 Karlyn Kohrs Campbell, *Man Cannot Speak for Her: A Critical Study of Early Feminist Rhetoric,* vol. 1 (Westport, CT: Greenwood Press, 1989), 9-10.

51 Ibid., 11.

52 Nancy Isenberg, *Sex and Citizenship in Antebellum America* (Chapel Hill: University of North Carolina Press, 1998), 44.

53 Mah, "Phantasies of the Public Sphere," 155.

Chapter 3: A Mixed Social Economy

1 Valverde, "The Mixed Social Economy," 33-34.

2 Ibid., 39.

3 Ibid., 44.

4 A notable exception is Jean-Marie Fecteau, *La liberté du pauvre: Crime et pauvreté au XIXe siècle québécois* (Montreal: VLB Éditeur, 2004) and Fecteau and Vaillancourt, "The Saint Vincent de Paul Society." See also Kevin Siena, "Hospitals for the Excluded or Convalescent Homes?: Workhouses, Medicalization and the Poor Law in Long Eighteenth-Century London and Pre-Confederation Toronto," *Canadian Bulletin of Medical History* 27, 1 (2010): 5-25.

5 Timothy Hasci, *Second Home: Orphan Asylums and Poor Families in America* (Cambridge, MA: Harvard University Press, 1997), 110.

6 Ibid.

7 Campbell, *A Mountain and a City,* 102.

8 Weaver, *Hamilton,* 56-57.

9 Parr, "The Welcome and the Wake," 110.

10 Clarke, *Piety and Nationalism,* 42.

11 "St. George's Report Committee Submitted to a Meeting Held in April, 1847," *Hamilton Herald,* September 12, 1908, Tinsley Hamilton Scrapbooks (THS), vol. 3, HPL; "How St. Andrew's Men Met Years Ago, The First Dinner of the Society Here in 1835 and What Transpired at It," *Hamilton Herald,* December 5, 1922, Herald Scrapbooks, vol. 2, pt. 1, HPL.

12 HAWHM, June 8, 1846, HPL.

13 HCCM, microfilm 107, vol. 5, September 10, 1849, 49-50, HPL.

14 HAWHM, May 5, 1847, HPL.

15 Parr, "The Welcome and the Wake," 105.

16 HAWHM, January 25, 1847; January 31, 1848, HPL.

17 Ibid., February 28, 1848.

18 Ibid.

19 HCCM, microfilm 105, vol. 2, January 13, 1847, 128, HPL.

20 HAWHM, February 22, 1847; May 5, 1847; June 14, 1848, HPL.

21 For a discussion of how reductions in outdoor relief forced more children into institutions see Priscilla F. Clement, *Welfare and the Poor in the Nineteenth-Century City:*

Philadelphia, 1800-1854 (Rutherford, NJ: Fairleigh Dickinson University Press, 1985), 119.

22 Splane, *Social Welfare in Ontario,* 221; Hasci, *Second Home,* 16; Michael Grossberg, *Governing the Hearth: Law and Family in Nineteenth-Century America* (Chapel Hill: University of North Carolina Press, 1985), 259-68; and LeRoy Ashby, *Endangered Children: Dependency, Neglect, and Abuse in American History* (New York: Twayne Publishers, 1997), 6-10.

23 Ivy Pinchbeck and Margaret Hewitt, *Children in English Society,* vol. 2, *From the Eighteenth Century to the Children Act 1948* (London: Routledge and Kegan Paul, 1973), 496.

24 Charlotte Neff, "Pauper Apprenticeship in Early Nineteenth Century Ontario," *Journal of Family History* 21, 2 (1996): 145-46.

25 HCCM, microfilm 105, vol. 4, January 29, 1849, 569-70, HPL.

26 Ibid., February 28, 1848, 293.

27 Ibid., March 6, 1848, 306.

28 Ibid., February 19, 1849, 604.

29 Ibid., microfilm 105, vol. 5, July 16, 1849, 6.

30 Ibid., microfilm 107, vol. 5, September 10, 1849, 49-50; July 16, 1849, 6; October 8, 1849, 70.

31 Donald Harman Akenson, *The Irish in Ontario: A Study in Rural History* (Montreal and Kingston: McGill-Queen's University Press, 1984), 29-30; Weaver, *Hamilton,* 57.

32 HCCM, microfilm 105, vol. 4, May 28, 1849, 686, HPL.

33 Campbell, *A Mountain and a City,* 105.

34 HCCM, microfilm 107, vol. 4, August 6, 1849, 23, HPL.

35 Ibid., vol. 5, August 20, 1849, 30-31.

36 Ibid.

37 Ibid., September 10, 1849, 49-50.

38 Ibid.

39 Katz, *People of Hamilton,* 63.

40 Clarke, *Piety and Nationalism,* 42.

41 Weaver, *Crimes, Constables, and Courts,* 49.

42 Ibid., 54.

43 Ibid., 57.

44 Paula Maurutto, *Governing Charities: Church and State in Toronto's Catholic Archdiocese 1850s to 1950s* (Montreal and Kingston: McGill-Queen's University Press, 2003), 20.

45 See for discussions G.S. Kealey, "Orangemen and the Corporation: The Politics of Class during the Union of the Canadas," in *Forging a Consensus: Historical Essays on Toronto,* ed. V.L. Russell (Toronto: University of Toronto Press, 1984), 41-86; Scott See, "The Orange Order and Social Violence in Mid-Nineteenth-Century Saint John," *Acadiensis* 13 (Autumn 1983): 68-92; and Rosalyn Trigger, "Irish Politics on Parade: The Clergy, National Societies, and St. Patrick's Day Processions in Nineteenth-Century Montreal and Toronto," *Histoire Sociale/Social History* 37, 74 (2004): 176-77.

46 Clarke, *Piety and Nationalism,* 39-40.

47 Ibid., 39.

48 HAWHM, March 25, 1850, HPL.

49 Ibid., emphasis in original.

50 Ibid., April 29, 1850.

51 Ibid., November 25, 1850.

52 Ibid., January 20, 1850; February 25, 1850; March 25, 1850; April 29, 1850; May 27, 1850; July 29, 1850; September 30, 1850; October 28, 1850.

53 Ibid., March 15, 1850; April 29, 1850.

54 Ibid., June 12, 1850.

55 Ibid.

Chapter 4: The City and the Ladies

1 Weaver, *Hamilton,* 56; Katz, *People of Hamilton,* 16.

2 Katz, *People of Hamilton,* 67.

3 HAWHM, June 12, 1850, HPL.

4 HCCM, microfilm 107, vol. 5, June 26, 1850, 226, HPL.

5 The Committee of Finance was "quite disposed to recommend an appropriation" if "a suitable site" was selected. Ibid., August 8, 1850, 257. The Committee on Schools subsequently recommended a lot in St. Mary's Ward, which was not approved by council. Ibid., October 16, 1850, 306.

6 Until the Married Women's Property Act was passed in Ontario in 1872, wives lacked legal rights to independent control over property brought into or acquired after their marriages. After the introduction of Courts of Chancery in 1837, married women could, under certain conditions, protect some property for themselves with the use of trusts. In 1859, married women in Ontario were granted the right to possess, but not manage or sell, property brought into their marriages or inherited after. Chambers, *Married Women and Property Law,* 7-9.

7 HAWHM, December 11, 1850, HPL.

8 Ibid., January 27, 1851.

9 Ibid.

10 Ibid., March 31, 1851.

11 Ibid., April 28, 1851.

12 Hasci, *Second Home,* 75.

13 Harvey, "The Protestant Orphan Asylum and the Montreal Ladies' Benevolent Society," 279.

14 HAWHM, October 27, 1851; June 30, 1851, HPL; HCCM, microfilm 108, vol. 6, January 28, 1852, 8, HPL.

15 HCCM, microfilm 108, vol. 6, January 28, 1852, 8, HPL. Thomas N. Best was an auctioneer, English, and Anglican. James Williams was a factory owner, American, and Presbyterian. William Distin was the chairman of the Board of Trustees for Common Schools, English, and an Anglican. Dennis Moore was a manufacturer, Upper Canadian, and a Methodist. Jasper Gilkison was a businessman, Upper Canadian, and Anglican. J.B. Dayfoot's biographical information is unknown. Edward Jackson was a manufacturer, American, and a Methodist. Canada, *Federal Census of 1871 (Ontario Index)* http://www.archives.ca/; Katz, *People of Hamilton,* 198-99; Bailey et al., eds., *Dictionary of Hamilton Biography,* s.v. "James Miller Williams," 211-12; ibid., s.v. "William Distin," 61; ibid., s.v. "Dennis Moore," 155-56; ibid., s.v. "Jasper Gilkison," 83; ibid., s.v. "Edward Jackson," 108-9.

16 Although J.B. Dayfoot's biographical information is unknown, he was very likely a Protestant since he became an ardent supporter and one of the Society's trustees later on.

17 HCCM, microfilm 108, vol. 6, February 4, 1852, 21, HPL.

18 Canada, *1851 Census Returns* (C-11762), 436.

19 C.J. Tracy, "Report of the Special Committee on Orphan Asylum," *Hamilton Spectator,* March 13, 1852.

20 HCCM, microfilm 108, vol. 6, February 4, 1852, 16-17, HPL. John Holden was a lawyer, born in England, and an Anglican. Bailey et al., eds., *Dictionary of Hamilton Biography*, s.v. "John Holden," 105.
21 The second Special Committee included C.J. Tracy, Charles Gray (biographical information unknown), Joseph Clement (biographical information unknown), Thomas Best (member of first Special Committee), and Dennis Moore (member of first Special Committee).
22 HAWHM, February 13, 1852, HPL, emphasis in original.
23 Ibid.
24 HCCM, microfilm 108, vol. 6, March 3, 1852, 33-34, HPL.
25 The vote was fourteen to four. Moore and Best voted against the conclusions of their own committee.
26 "The Orphan Asylum," *Hamilton Spectator*, March 13, 1852.
27 HCCM, microfilm 108, vol. 6, March 10, 1852, 36-37, HPL.
28 See HAWHM, June 28, 1848, HPL.
29 John Fisher, John Young, Edward Jackson, and E. Cartwright Thomas, "Memorial of the Building Committee," *Hamilton Spectator*, March 13, 1852.
30 Ibid.
31 Ibid.
32 Cecilia Morgan, *Public Men and Virtuous Women: The Gendered Languages of Religion and Politics in Upper Canada, 1791-1850* (Toronto: University of Toronto Press, 1996), 197.
33 Fisher et al., "Memorial of the Building Committee."
34 "Proceedings of the City Council," *Hamilton Spectator*, March 17, 1852, emphasis in original.
35 Ibid.
36 "Petition for a Grant," *Hamilton Spectator*, March 13, 1852.
37 Ibid.
38 Although the editorial columns in the *Spectator* were unsigned, it is reasonable to assume that Smiley was the author. Unfortunately, issues of the *Canadian* for this period are not extant, but some information can be gleaned from Smiley's responses.
39 For biographical information see Bailey et al., eds., *Dictionary of Hamilton Biography*, s.v. "Robert Smiley," 182-83.
40 "The Orphan Asylum," *Hamilton Spectator*, March 20, 1852.
41 "'The Sectarian Struggle,'" *Hamilton Spectator*, March 24, 1852.
42 HCCM, microfilm 108, vol. 6, March 15, 1852, 41, HPL.
43 HAWHM, February 22, 1852, HPL.
44 "Proceedings of the City Council," *Hamilton Spectator*, April 3, 1852.
45 Habermas, *The Structural Transformation of the Public Sphere*, 56, 86-87.
46 "Proceedings of the City Council," *Hamilton Spectator*, April 3, 1852.
47 Valverde, "The Mixed Social Economy," 39-40.
48 HCCM, microfilm 110, vol. 9, January 27, 1862, 438, HPL. David Burley discusses a strikingly similar case in *A Particular Condition in Life: Self-Employment and Social Mobility in Mid-Victorian Brantford, Ontario* (Montreal and Kingston: McGill-Queen's University Press, 1994), 224-25.
49 "Proceedings of the City Council," *Hamilton Spectator*, April 3, 1852.
50 HCCM, microfilm 108, vol. 6, March 31, 1852, 49, HPL.
51 HAWHM, March 29, 1852, HPL.
52 Ibid., April 5, 1852.

53 "The Orphan Asylum," *Hamilton Spectator,* April 7, 1852.
54 Ibid.
55 Ibid.
56 Ibid.
57 HAWHM, April 26, 1852, HPL.
58 "St. Mary's Orphanage: Its Origin and Growth," Sisters of St. Joseph's Convent Records, Hamilton, ON.
59 HAWHM, Annual Treasurer's Reports, 1861-71, HPL.

Chapter 5: Public Acts and Private Lives

1 HAWHM, May 10, 1852, HPL.
2 Fecteau and Vaillancourt, "The Saint Vincent de Paul Society," 201.
3 Ibid., 200.
4 Ryan, *The Cradle of the Middle Class.*
5 Suzanne Lebsock, *The Free Women of Petersburg: Status and Culture in a Southern Town, 1784-1860* (New York: W.W. Norton, 1984), 198.
6 Jan Noel, "Women and Social Welfare in the Montreal Region, 1800-1833: Preliminary Findings," in *Changing Roles of Women with the Christian Church in Canada,* ed. Elizabeth G. Muir and Marilyn F. Whiteley (Toronto: University of Toronto Press, 1995), 278.
7 Lebsock, *Free Women of Petersburg,* 197.
8 News clipping from the *Hamilton Spectator,* May 8, 1957, Sisters of St. Joseph Scrapbook, vol. 1, HPL. The act was reprinted in 1957 from an original newspaper report for which no date was given. Although I have been unable to locate this act in the statutes, the exact same language was used in the Act to incorporate the Sisters of St. Joseph for the Diocese of Toronto, in Upper Canada, Statutes of the Province of Canada, ch. 225 (1855), 969-71.
9 Act to incorporate the Children's Industrial School of the City of Hamilton, Statutes of the Province of Canada, ch. 145 (1864), 612-14.
10 Act to incorporate the Trustees of *The Hamilton Orphan Asylum,* Statutes of the Province of Canada, ch. 67 (1852), 244-47. The 1864 act to incorporate Hamilton's Children's Industrial School directed the school to forward its reports to "the Governor and both Houses of the Provincial Parliament."
11 For a discussion of technologies of government, see Nikolas Rose and Peter Miller, "Political Power beyond the State: Problematics of Government," *British Journal of Sociology* 43, 2 (1992): 173-205; and Graham Burchell, Colin Gordon, and Peter Miller, eds., *The Foucault Effect: Studies in Governmentality* (Chicago: Chicago University Press, 1991).
12 Act to incorporate the Trustees of *The Hamilton Orphan Asylum,* 245-46.
13 Neff, "Pauper Apprenticeship," 149; Splane, *Social Welfare in Ontario,* 221.
14 For a discussion, see Grossberg, *Governing the Hearth,* 266-68.
15 Ibid., 264-65.
16 Ibid., 266-68.
17 Ibid., 234.
18 Although Grossberg identifies "republicanism" as the ideological basis for changes in custody law, liberal philosophical principles of the individual and natural-born rights are fundamental to this particular vision of family. While the terms republican and liberal are hardly interchangeable, Grossberg's terminology betrays more about notions of American exceptionalism than philosophical differences between the two ideologies in this particular case. For an analysis of the paradigmatic shift in familial ideology

over the colonial and early American period from a "Filmerian" to a "Lockean" system, see Mary Beth Norton, *Founding Mothers and Fathers: Gendered Power and the Forming of American Society* (New York: A.A. Knopf, 1996).

19 Hasci, *Second Home*, 1.

20 Neff, "The Role of Protestant Children's Homes," 59.

21 Ibid.

22 Patricia T. Rooke and R.L. Schnell, "Childhood and Charity in Nineteenth-Century British North America," *Histoire Sociale/Social History* 15, 29 (1982): 167-69.

23 Harvey, "The Protestant Orphan Asylum," 156-57.

24 Grossberg, *Governing the Hearth*, 241-47; Splane, *Social Welfare in Ontario*, 254-55.

25 Splane, *Social Welfare in Ontario*, 254-55.

26 Pinchbeck and Hewitt, *Children in English Society*, 382.

27 Neff, "Pauper Apprenticeship," 150.

28 News clipping from the *Hamilton Spectator*, May 8, 1957, Sisters of St. Joseph Scrapbook, vol. 1, HPL.

29 Martin J. O'Dea, "Annual Report of the St. Mary's Orphan Asylum," *Hamilton Spectator*, February 6, 1865.

30 Act to incorporate the Children's Industrial School of the City of Hamilton, 614.

31 Hasci, *Second Home*, 56.

32 See as examples Judith Fingard, *The Dark Side of Life in Victorian Halifax* (Halifax, NS: Pottersfield Press, 1989); Bettina Bradbury, "The Fragmented Family: Family Strategies in the Face of Death, Illness, and Poverty," in *Childhood and Family in Canadian History*, ed. Joy Parr (Toronto: McClelland and Stewart Limited, 1982), 109-28; Charlotte Neff, "The Role of Protestant Children's Homes," 48-88.

33 Hasci, *Second Home*, 3.

34 Ibid., 144.

35 Bruce Bellingham, "Institution and Family: An Alternative View of Nineteenth-Century Child Saving," *Social Problems* 33, 6 (1986): 49.

36 Ibid., 51.

37 For a discussion, see Susan Whitelaw Downs and Michael W. Sherraden, "The Orphan Asylum in the Nineteenth Century," *Social Service Review* 57, 2 (1983): 272-90.

38 Katz, *People of Hamilton*, 21.

39 Peter Mandler, "Poverty and Charity in the Nineteenth-Century Metropolis: An Introduction," in *The Uses of Charity: The Poor on Relief in the Nineteenth-Century Metropolis*, ed. Peter Mandler (Philadelphia: University of Pennsylvania Press, 1990), 3.

40 Ibid.

41 O'Dea, "Annual Report of the St. Mary's Orphan Asylum."

42 Neff, "The Role of Protestant Children's Homes," 59.

43 HAWHM, December 28, 1863, HPL.

44 Ibid., March 25, 1867.

45 Ibid., June 29, 1868.

46 O'Dea, "Annual Report of the St. Mary's Orphan Asylum."

47 Neff, "The Role of Protestant Children's Homes," 59.

48 HAWHM, August 26, 1854, HPL.

49 Ibid., January 27, 1872; April 29, 1872.

50 Ibid., August 26, 1872.

51 Ibid., December 28, 1868.

52 Ibid., April 24, 1865.

53 Hasci, *Second Home*, 126.

54 Rooke and Schnell, "Childhood and Charity," 167-69.
55 "The Industrial School," *Hamilton Spectator,* May 6, 1865.
56 HAWHM, June 29, 1857, HPL.
57 Ibid., October 20, 1858.
58 Ibid., July 29, 1867.
59 Ibid.
60 Ibid., August 26, 1867.
61 Ibid., February 28, 1870.
62 Ibid., October 30, 1865.
63 For an illuminating exploration of affective relationships between asylum children and their parents in late nineteenth-century America, see Judith A. Dulberger, *"Mother Donit fore the Best": Correspondence of a Nineteenth-Century Orphan Asylum* (Syracuse, NY: Syracuse University Press, 1996).
64 HAWHM, November 29, 1858, HPL.
65 Ibid., December 27, 1858.
66 Ibid., October 28, 1867; December 27, 1869.
67 Ibid., December 28, 1868; September 26, 1870.
68 Neff, "Role of Protestant Children's Homes," 49.
69 Harvey, "The Protestant Orphan Asylum," 192-93.
70 Lawes, *Women and Reform,* 136-39.
71 Neff, "Role of Protestant Children's Homes," 49.
72 Constance Backhouse, "Shifting Patterns in Nineteenth-Century Canadian Custody Law," in *Essays in the History of Canadian Law,* vol. 1, ed. David H. Flaherty (Toronto: Osgoode Society, 1981), 215.
73 Grossberg, *Governing the Hearth,* 235.
74 Backhouse, "Shifting Patterns," 227.
75 HAWHM, June 29, 1847, HPL.
76 Ibid., August 25, 1879; November 10, 1879.
77 Ibid., November 24, 1879.
78 Ibid., March 31, 1862.
79 Ibid., November 30, 1863.
80 Ibid., November 26, 1866.
81 Grossberg, *Governing the Hearth,* 236.
82 Ibid., 237.
83 Backhouse, "Shifting Patterns," 230.
84 Ibid., 240-41.

Chapter 6: Institutional Care, Adoption, and Apprenticeship

1 Matthew A. Crenson, *Building the Invisible Orphanage: A Prehistory of the American Welfare System* (Cambridge, MA: Harvard University Press, 1998), 19, 37; Hasci, *Second Home,* 20; David J. Rothman, *The Discovery of the Asylum: Social Order and Disorder in the New Republic* (Boston: Little, Brown and Co., 1971), 206; Susan Houston, "Impetus to Reform: Urban Crime, Poverty and Ignorance in Ontario, 1850-1875" (PhD diss., University of Toronto, 1974), 268, 285.
2 For discussion of these discourses, see Xiaobei Chen, *Tending the Gardens of Citizenship: Child Saving in Toronto 1880s-1920s* (Toronto: University of Toronto Press, 2005).
3 HAWHM, January 29, 1862, HPL.
4 Ibid., February 5, 1857.
5 Neff, "Role of Protestant Children's Homes," 62.

6 Ibid., 75.

7 Ibid., 60.

8 For example, Margaret Brown was a resident of the asylum in 1862 and identified as an "idiot." She remained in the asylum until 1876, when she was removed to the Wentworth County Jail. Lily Wade and Mary Hannigan, both of whom were blind, were also long-time residents of the home. HAWHM, October 27, 1862; August 15, 1876, HPL.

9 Ibid., April 25, 1859; July 27, 1863; September 26, 1864.

10 Ibid., February 28, 1870.

11 Ibid., April 30, 1849; November 27, 1865.

12 Ibid., February 28, 1870. The secretary of the HOA tabulated admissions, discharges, deaths, and the number of children in the house on 31 December from 1848 to 1869 at the request of Stanislas Drapeau.

13 Mary Anne, the Wilsons' daughter, helped around the house regularly. One son died in the summer of 1865 and two other boys were mentioned in the asylum records. Ibid., March 25, 1867.

14 Ibid., June 26, 1848; June 25, 1849. In contrast, Timothy Hasci found that in most American asylums the superintendent's wife "usually functioned as an unpaid matron." Hasci, *Second Home,* 81.

15 Kathleen McCarthy observed a similar pattern in Chicago's early orphan asylums. Kathleen D. McCarthy, *Noblesse Oblige: Charity and Cultural Philanthropy in Chicago, 1849-1929* (Chicago: University of Chicago Press, 1982), 8.

16 HAWHM, December 31, 1866, HPL.

17 Ibid., June 12, 1876.

18 Ibid., September 26, 1859.

19 Ibid., July 26, 1862.

20 Ibid., October 28, 1867.

21 Ibid., June 29, 1868.

22 Ibid., April 11, 1876.

23 See for discussion, Barbara Welter, "The Cult of True Womanhood, 1820-1860," *American Quarterly* 18 (Summer 1966): 151-75; Kathryn Kish Sklar, *Catharine Beecher: A Study in American Domesticity* (New York: W.W. Norton and Company, 1976); Ryan, *Cradle of the Middle Class;* Davidoff and Hall, *Family Fortunes;* Ruth H. Bloch, "American Feminine Ideals in Transition: The Rise of the Moral Mother, 1785-1815," *Feminist Studies* 4 (1978): 101-26; Steven Mintz and Susan Kellogg, *Domestic Revolutions: A Social History of American Family Life* (New York: Free Press, 1988), 54-55, 59; Errington, *Wives and Mothers*; Van Die, *An Evangelical Mind.*

24 See for discussion Davidoff and Hall, *Family Fortunes,* esp. 395-98; Errington, *Wives and Mothers,* chp. 6; Yeo, *Contest for Social Science,* 63, 72; and, for specific reference to school routine and organization, Susan Houston and Alison Prentice, *Schooling and Scholars in Nineteenth-Century Ontario* (Toronto: University of Toronto Press, 1988), 192.

25 HAWHM, June 28, 1848, HPL.

26 See Susan Porter, "The Benevolent Asylum – Image and Reality: The Care and Training of Female Orphans in Boston, 1800-1840," (PhD diss., Boston University, 1984), 135-36.

27 Sophia MacNab qtd. in Houston and Prentice, *Schooling and Scholars,* 10.

28 Charlotte Neff, "The Education of Destitute Homeless Children in Nineteenth-Century Ontario," *Journal of Family History* 29, 1 (2004): 4.

29 Ibid., 26.

30 Houston and Prentice, *Schooling and Scholars,* 99, 101.
31 HAWHM, June 28, 1848, HPL.
32 Ibid., May 30, 1853. For a discussion of the social composition of students who entered the Hamilton Central School and the ultimate failure of the "egalitarian aims expressed by its promoters," see Ian E. Davey, "School Reform and School Attendance: The Hamilton Central School, 1853-1861," in *Education and Social Change: Themes from Ontario's Past,* ed. Michael B. Katz and Paul H. Mattingly (New York: New York University Press, 1975), 294-314.
33 Houston and Prentice, *Schooling and Scholars,* 79.
34 Hasci, *Second Home,* 176.
35 Harvey, "The Protestant Orphan Asylum," 180.
36 Neff, "The Education of Destitute Homeless Children," 13.
37 R.D. Gidney, "Ryerson, Egerton," *Dictionary of Canadian Biography Online,* vol. 11, http://www.biographi.ca/en/bio/ryerson_egerton_11E.html.
38 HAWHM, June 28, 1848, HPL; Houston and Prentice, *Schooling and Scholars,* 118-19.
39 Houston and Prentice, *Schooling and Scholars,* 118-19.
40 HAWHM, March 21, 1860, HPL, emphasis in original.
41 Houston and Prentice, *Schooling and Scholars,* 71.
42 Ibid., 112.
43 HAWHM, June 26, 1848, HPL.
44 Houston and Prentice, *Schooling and Scholars,* 75.
45 Hasci, *Second Home,* 173.
46 See Neil Semple, "'The Nurture and Admonition of the Lord': Nineteenth-Century Canadian Methodism's Response to Childhood," *Histoire Sociale/Social History* 14, 27 (1981): 163-65. In contrast, see Van Die, *An Evangelical Mind,* 181.
47 HAWHM, June 28, 1848, HPL.
48 Ibid., June 26, 1871.
49 Ibid., June 12, 1876.
50 Ibid., March 21, 1860.
51 Ibid., September 25, 1865.
52 Katz, *People of Hamilton,* 57.
53 Ibid., 60.
54 Patricia T. Rooke and R.L. Schnell, "Guttersnipes and Charity Children: Nineteenth Century Child Rescue in the Atlantic Provinces," in *Studies in Childhood History: A Canadian Perspective,* ed. Patricia T. Rooke and R.L. Schnell (Calgary: Detselig Enterprises Limited, 1982), 94.
55 Hasci, *Second Home,* 173-74.
56 Harvey, "The Protestant Orphan Asylum," 182-83.
57 Hasci, *Second Home,* 197.
58 HAWHM, January 28, 1867, HPL.
59 Ibid., December 27, 1869.
60 Ibid., July 25, 1859.
61 Ibid., July 25, 1864.
62 Mintz and Kellogg, *Domestic Revolutions,* 48-49.
63 HAWHM, August 26, 1867, HPL.
64 Ibid., September 30, 1867.
65 Ibid., November 30, 1868.
66 Ibid., January n.d., 1881.

67 Hasci, *Second Home,* 155.
68 Harvey, "The Protestant Orphan Asylum," 173.
69 Houston and Prentice, *Schooling and Scholars,* 194.
70 Mintz and Kellogg, *Domestic Revolutions,* 58-59. See also Ashby, *Endangered Children,* 20.
71 For a discussion of the broad contours of adoption practice in nineteenth- and twentieth-century English Canada see Strong-Boag, *Finding Families, Finding Ourselves.*
72 Joseph Ben-Or, "The Law of Adoption in the United States: Its Massachusetts Origins and the Statute of 1851," *New England Historical and Genealogical Register* 130 (1976): 259-73.
73 Grossberg, *Governing the Hearth,* 271-72.
74 Ibid., 280. See also Susan Porter, "A Good Home: Indenture and Adoption in Nineteenth-Century Orphanages," in *Adoption in America: Historical Perspectives,* ed. E. Wayne Carp (Ann Arbor: University of Michigan Press, 2002), 27-50.
75 E. Wayne Carp, Introduction to *Adoption in America: Historical Perspectives,* 3.
76 Peter W. Ward, "Unwed Motherhood in Nineteenth-Century English Canada," *Historical Papers* (1981): 53; Splane, *Social Welfare in Ontario,* 225.
77 HAWHM, February 14, 1854; June 30, 1862, HPL.
78 Samuel Wilson explained to a government agent who inspected the asylum in September 1864 that children were adopted from the institution from infancy to five years. Ibid., September 26, 1864.
79 Neff, "Pauper Apprenticeship," 157.
80 HAWHM, March 30, 1863, HPL.
81 Ibid., December 8, 1879.
82 Ibid., June 12, 1862; June 30, 1862.
83 Ibid., September 28, 1863.
84 Ibid., December 30, 1867.
85 Ibid., April 25, 1859; January 29, 1863; July 27, 1863.
86 Rooke and Schnell, "Childhood and Charity," 174-75.
87 HAWHM, September 28, 1868, HPL, emphasis in original.
88 Grossberg, *Governing the Hearth,* 276-78.
89 See Joy Parr, *Labouring Children: British Immigrant Apprentices to Canada, 1869-1924* (Montreal and Kingston: McGill-Queen's University Press, 1980).
90 Sutherland, *Children in English-Canadian Society,* 6, 10.
91 HAWHM, July 31, 1854; August 26, 1854, HPL.
92 Ibid., November 29, 1858.
93 Ibid., June 26, 1866.
94 Neff, "Pauper Apprenticeship," 157.
95 HAWHM, January n.d., 1881, HPL.
96 Ibid., July 27, 1863.
97 Ibid., September 30, 1872.
98 Ibid., March 30, 1863.
99 Ibid., April 27, 1868.
100 Ibid., June 10, 1878.

Chapter 7: Continuity and Change, 1870-93

1 Bryan D. Palmer, *A Culture in Conflict: Skilled Workers and Industrial Capitalism in Hamilton, Ontario, 1860-1914* (Montreal and Kingston: McGill-Queen's University Press, 1979), 9, 15.
2 Ibid., 10; Katz, *People of Hamilton,* 179, 192.

3 Katz, *People of Hamilton*, 79-80, 82.
4 Palmer, *Culture in Conflict*, 15.
5 Katz, *People of Hamilton*, 87-88.
6 Palmer, *Culture in Conflict*, 17.
7 HAWHM, November 6, 1872, HPL.
8 Bryan D. Palmer, *Working-Class Experience: The Rise and Reconstitution of Canadian Labour, 1800-1980* (Toronto: Butterworth and Co., 1983), 82.
9 HAWHM, November 8, 1871, HPL.
10 "Twenty-Ninth Annual Report of the Hamilton Orphan Asylum and Ladies' Benevolent Society," *Hamilton Spectator*, October 2, 1875.
11 HAWHM, October 1878, HPL.
12 Charlotte Neff, "Government Approaches to Child Neglect and Mistreatment in Nineteenth-Century Ontario," *Histoire Sociale/Social History* 41, 81 (2008): 181.
13 Ibid.
14 Ibid., 181-82.
15 Ibid., 182.
16 Splane, *Social Welfare in Ontario*, 57.
17 Peter Oliver, "Langmuir, John Woodburn, *Dictionary of Canadian Biography Online*, vol. 14, http://www.biographi.ca/en/bio/langmuir_john_woodburn_14E.html.
18 Splane, *Social Welfare in Ontario*, 56-64.
19 Curtis, *True Government*, 11.
20 J.W. Langmuir, qtd in Splane, *Social Welfare in Ontario*, 57.
21 Neff, "Government Approaches," 198. See also Maurutto, *Governing Charities*, 35.
22 Curtis, *True Government*, 7.
23 HAWHM, August 31, 1874, HPL.
24 Ibid., September 23, 1875.
25 Ibid., September 27, 1875.
26 Splane, *Social Welfare in Ontario*, 89, 92-94.
27 HAWHM, March 28, 1869, HPL.
28 Ibid., January 31, 1876.
29 Ibid., May 31, 1875.
30 Ibid., June 26, 1876.
31 Ibid., September 29, 1876.
32 Ibid.
33 Ibid., November 6, 1872.
34 Ibid., February 15, 1877; April 30, 1877; September 30, 1878.
35 Ibid., January n.d., 1880.
36 Ibid., June 11, 1877; July 29, 1878; January 28, 1884; January 13, 1889.
37 Ibid., July 12, 1880; January 18, 1887.
38 Neff, "Government Approaches," 196.
39 "Annual Meeting of the Orphan Asylum and Aged Women's Home," *Hamilton Spectator*, October 5, 1881; HAWHM, February 27, 1883; October 29, 1883, HPL.
40 HAWHM, March 13, 1882; September 23, 1883; January 18, 1887; June 8, 1889, HPL.
41 There is no evidence to suggest that trustees played any role in the writing of annual reports. Newspaper coverage indicates that members of the executive read out the annual reports at public meetings. See as examples "Annual Meeting of the Orphan Asylum and Aged Women's Home," *Hamilton Spectator*, October 5, 1881; "The Annual Report and General Meeting Yesterday," *Hamilton Spectator*, October 8, 1884.

42 HAWHM, January 1, 1882; October 30, 1882; March 27, 1886; May 13, 1887; June 10, 1889; October 28, 1889; January 27, 1890, HPL.
43 "The Annual Report and General Meeting Yesterday," *Hamilton Spectator,* October 8, 1884.
44 "The Orphan Asylum. Annual Report of the Home on Wellington Street," *Hamilton Spectator,* October 8, 1883.
45 HAWHM, October 1, 1894, HPL.
46 Ibid., September 29, 1875.
47 Hamilton City Directories, 1881-86, HPL.
48 Splane, *Social Welfare in Ontario,* 114. For a discussion, see Michael B. Katz, *In the Shadow of the Poorhouse: A Social History of Welfare in America* (New York: Basic Books, 1996), 58-84.
49 HAWHM, October 6, 1891, HPL.
50 Ibid., November 30, 1891.
51 Ibid., June 27, 1892.
52 Ibid., October 4, 1892.
53 Splane, *Social Welfare in Ontario,* 115.
54 HAWHM, February 26, 1894, HPL.
55 Ibid., October 1, 1896.
56 Ibid., September 28, 1896.
57 Ibid., October 1, 1896.
58 Ibid., February 23, 1903.
59 For discussion, see Splane, *Social Welfare in Ontario,* 259-60; Patricia Rooke and R.L. Schnell, "The Rise and Decline of British North American Protestant Orphan's Homes as Woman's Domain, 1850-1930," *Atlantis* 7, 2 (1982): 21-35; Bullen, "J.J. Kelso and the 'New' Child-Savers," 107-28; and Strong-Boag, *Fostering Nation?*
60 Bullen, "J. J. Kelso and the 'New' Child-Savers," 112. For a thorough discussion of the decline of orphanages in the United States, see Crenson, *Building the Invisible Orphanage.*
61 For discussion about Kelso's influence on late nineteenth-century child welfare policies, see Jones and Rutman, *In the Children's Aid;* Bullen, "J.J. Kelso and the 'New' Child-Savers"; and Rooke and Schnell, *Discarding the Asylum.*
62 Bullen, "J.J. Kelso and the 'New' Child-Savers," 111.
63 Ibid.
64 Ibid., 116.
65 Ibid., 114.
66 Ibid., 115.
67 HAWHM, October n.d., 1894, HPL.
68 Bullen, "J.J. Kelso and the 'New' Child-Savers," 117.
69 HAWHM, October 14, 1895, HPL.
70 Ibid., September 27, 1902.
71 Ibid., December 29, 1913.
72 Bullen, "J.J. Kelso and the 'New' Child-Savers," 110; Neff, "Government Approaches," 213-14.
73 HAWHM, October n.d., 1894, HPL.
74 Bullen, "J.J. Kelso and the 'New' Child-Savers," 123.
75 Nancy Christie, *Engendering the State: Family, Work and Welfare in Canada* (Toronto: University of Toronto Press, 2000), 32-33.
76 Ibid., 31.

Conclusion: A Career in Christian Charity

1 HAWHM, Newspaper clipping inserted at May 31, 1875, HPL. Although this obituary was unsigned, its phrasing is almost identical to passages in Nathanael Burwash's eulogy in the *Canadian Methodist Magazine,* which leaves little doubt that he was the author.

2 Burwash, "Edward and Lydia Jackson," part II, 103-4.

3 Habermas, *The Structural Transformation of the Public Sphere,* 142.

4 Denise Riley, *"Am I That Name?" Feminism and the Category of "Women" in History* (London: Macmillan Press, 1988), 48-51.

5 See Christie, *Engendering the State;* Linda Gordon, *Pitied but Not Entitled: Single Mothers and the History of Welfare: 1890-1935* (New York: Free Press, 1994); Margaret Jane Hillyard Little, *"No Car, No Radio, No Liquor Permit": The Moral Regulation of Single Mothers in Ontario, 1920-1997* (Toronto: Oxford University Press, 1998); Theda Skocpol, *Protecting Soldiers and Mothers: The Political Origins of Social Policy in the United States* (Cambridge, MA: Belknap Press of Harvard University Press, 1992).

6 Paula Baker, "The Domestication of Politics: Women and American Political Society, 1780-1920," *American Historical Review* 89, 3 (June 1984): 640.

7 Ibid., 642.

8 See Seth Koven and Sonya Michel, eds., *Mothers of a New World: Maternalist Politics and the Origins of Welfare States* (New York: Routledge, 1993) and Marian van der Klein et al., eds., *Maternalism Reconsidered: Motherhood, Welfare and Social Policy in the Twentieth Century* (New York: Berghahn Books, 2012).

Bibliography

Primary Sources

Hamilton Aged Women's Home Minutes (HAWHM). 1846-1915. Hamilton Public Library.

Hamilton City Council Minutes (HCCM). 1847-62. Hamilton Public Library.

Hamilton City Directories. 1881-86. Hamilton Public Library.

Herald Scrapbooks, vol. 2, pt. 1. Hamilton Public Library.

Sisters of St. Joseph Scrapbook, vol. 1. Hamilton Public Library.

"St. Mary's Orphanage: Its Origin and Growth." Sisters of St. Joseph's Convent Records, Hamilton, ON.

Tinsley Hamilton Scrapbooks, vols. 3-4. Hamilton Public Library.

Newspapers

Dundas Weekly Post, November 21, 1834.

Gore Gazette, June 9, 1827.

Hamilton Spectator, July 21, 1847; March 13, 1852; March 17, 1852; March 20, 1852; March 24, 1852; April 3, 1852; April 7, 1852; February 6, 1865; May 6, 1865; October 2, 1875; October 5, 1881; October 8, 1883; October 8, 1884.

Western Mercury (Hamilton), April 24, 1834.

Government Documents

Act to alter and amend the Act incorporating the Town of Hamilton, and to erect the same into a City. Statutes of the Province of Canada. Chapter 73 (1846): 981-1005.

Act to incorporate the Children's Industrial School of the City of Hamilton. Statutes of the Province of Canada. Chapter 145 (1864): 612-14.

Act to incorporate the Sisters of St. Joseph for the Diocese of Toronto, in Upper Canada. Statutes of the Province of Canada. Chapter 225 (1855): 969-71.

Act to incorporate the Trustees of *The Hamilton Orphan Asylum.* Statutes of the Province of Canada. Chapter 67 (1852): 244-47.

Canada. *1851 Census Returns* (C-11762).

Canada. *Federal Census of 1871 (Ontario Index).* http://www.archives.ca/.

Secondary Sources

Acheson, T.W. "Evangelicals and Public Life in Southern New Brunswick, 1830-1880." In *Religion and Public Life in Canada: Historical and Comparative Perspectives,* edited by Marguerite Van Die, 50-68. Toronto: University of Toronto Press, 2001.

Akenson, Donald Harman. *The Irish in Ontario: A Study in Rural History.* Kingston and Montreal: McGill-Queen's University Press, 1984.

Andrew, Donna T. *Philanthropy and Police: London Charity in the Eighteenth Century.* Princeton, NJ: Princeton University Press, 1989.

Arendt, Hannah. *The Human Condition.* 2nd ed. Chicago: University of Chicago Press, 1998.

Ariès, Phillip. *Centuries of Childhood: A Social History of Family Life.* New York: Knopf, 1962.

Ashby, LeRoy. *Endangered Children: Dependency, Neglect, and Abuse in American History.* New York: Twayne Publishers, 1997.

Backhouse, Constance. "Married Women's Property Law in Nineteenth-Century Canada." *Law and History Review* 6, 2 (1988): 211-57.

–. "Shifting Patterns in Nineteenth-Century Canadian Custody Law." In *Essays in the History of Canadian Law,* vol. 1, edited by David H. Flaherty, 212-48. Toronto: Osgoode Society, 1981.

Baehre, Rainer. "Paupers and Poor Relief in Upper Canada." In *Historical Essays on Upper Canada: New Perspectives,* edited by James Keith Johnson and Bruce G. Wilson, 305-40. Ottawa: Carleton University Press, 1989.

Bailey, Thomas Melville, Patricia Filer, Robert L. Fraser, and John C. Weaver, eds. *Dictionary of Hamilton Biography.* Vol. 1. Hamilton: W.L. Griffin Limited, 1981.

Baker, Paula. "The Domestication of Politics: Women and American Political Society, 1780-1920." *American Historical Review* 89, 3 (1984): 620-47.

Bamman, Haley P. "The Ladies Benevolent Society of Hamilton, Ontario: Form and Function in Mid-Nineteenth Century Urban Philanthropy." In *The Canadian Social History Project, Interim Report No. 4,* edited by Michael B. Katz, 162-217. Toronto: Department of History and Philosophy of Education, Ontario Institute for Studies in Education, 1972.

Bellingham, Bruce. "Institution and Family: An Alternative View of Nineteenth-Century Child Saving." *Social Problems* 33, 6 (1986): 33-57.

Benhabib, Seyla. "Models of Public Space: Hannah Arendt, the Liberal Tradition, and Jurgen Habermas." In *Feminism, the Public and the Private,* edited by Joan B. Landes, 65-99. Oxford: Oxford University Press, 1998.

Ben-Or, Joseph. "The Law of Adoption in the United States: Its Massachusetts Origins and the Statute of 1851." *New England Historical and Genealogical Register* 130 (1976): 259-73.

Berg, Barbara. *The Remembered Gate: Origins of American Feminism, the Woman and the City, 1800-1860.* New York: Oxford University Press, 1978.

Bloch, Ruth H. "American Feminine Ideals in Transition: The Rise of the Moral Mother, 1785-1815." *Feminist Studies* 4 (1978): 101-26.

Boylan, Anne M. *The Origins of Women's Activism: New York and Boston, 1797-1840.* Chapel Hill: University of North Carolina Press, 2002.

Bradbury, Bettina. "The Fragmented Family: Family Strategies in the Face of Death, Illness, and Poverty." In *Childhood and Family in Canadian History,* edited by Joy Parr, 109-28. Toronto: McClelland and Stewart Limited, 1982.

–. "Women at the Hustings: Gender, Citizenship, and the Montreal By-Elections of 1832." In *Rethinking Canada: The Promise of Women's History,* 5th ed., edited by Mona Gleason and Adele Perry, 73-94. Toronto: Oxford University Press Canada, 2006.

Bullen, John. "J.J. Kelso and the 'New' Child-Savers: The Genesis of the Children's Aid Movement in Ontario." *Ontario History* 82, 2 (1990): 107-28.

Burchell, Graham, Colin Gordon, and Peter Miller, eds. *The Foucault Effect: Studies in Governmentality.* Chicago: Chicago University Press, 1991.

Burley, David. *A Particular Condition in Life: Self-Employment and Social Mobility in Mid-Victorian Brantford, Ontario.* Montreal and Kingston: McGill-Queen's University Press, 1994.

Burwash, Nathanael. "Edward and Lydia Ann Jackson." Part I. *Canadian Methodist Magazine, Devoted to Religion, Literature, and Social Progress* 3, 1 (January 1876): 1-10.

–. "Edward and Lydia Ann Jackson." Part II. *Canadian Methodist Magazine, Devoted to Religion, Literature, and Social Progress* 3, 2 (February 1876): 97-104.

Campbell, Karlyn Kohrs. *Man Cannot Speak for Her: A Critical Study of Early Feminist Rhetoric.* Vol. 1. Westport, CT: Greenwood Press, 1989.

Campbell, Marjorie. *A Mountain and a City: The Story of Hamilton.* Toronto: McClelland and Stewart, 1966.

Carp, E. Wayne. Introduction to *Adoption in America: Historical Perspectives,* edited by E. Wayne Carp, 1-26. Ann Arbor: University of Michigan Press, 2002.

Chambers, Lori. *Married Women and Property Law in Victorian Ontario.* Toronto: University of Toronto Press, 1997.

Chen, Xiaobei. *Tending the Gardens of Citizenship: Child Saving in Toronto 1880s-1920s.* Toronto: University of Toronto Press, 2005.

Christie, Nancy. *Engendering the State: Family, Work, and Welfare in Canada.* Toronto: University of Toronto Press, 2000.

Clarke, Brian P. *Piety and Nationalism: Lay Voluntary Associations and the Creation of an Irish-Catholic Community in Toronto, 1850-1895.* Montreal and Kingston: McGill-Queen's University Press, 1993.

Clement, Priscilla F. *Welfare and the Poor in the Nineteenth-Century City: Philadelphia, 1800-1854.* Rutherford, NJ: Fairleigh Dickinson University Press, 1985.

Constant, Jean-François, and Michel Ducharme, eds. *Liberalism and Hegemony: Debating the Liberal Revolution.* Toronto: University of Toronto Press, 2009.

Cook, Sharon Anne. *Through Sunshine and Shadow: The Woman's Christian Temperance Union, Evangelicalism, and Reform in Ontario, 1874-1930.* Montreal and Kingston: McGill-Queen's University Press, 1995.

Corrigan, Philip, and Derek Sayer. *The Great Arch: English State Formation as Cultural Revolution.* Oxford: Basil Blackwell, 1985.

Cott, Nancy. *The Bonds of Womanhood: Woman's Sphere in New England, 1780-1835.* New Haven, CT: Yale University Press, 1977.

Crenson, Matthew A. *Building the Invisible Orphanage: A Prehistory of the American Welfare System.* Cambridge, MA: Harvard University Press, 1998.

Cunningham, Hugh. Introduction to *Charity, Philanthropy and Reform From the 1690s to 1850,* edited by Hugh Cunningham and Joanna Innes, 1-14. London: Macmillan Press Limited, 1998.

Curtis, Bruce. *The Politics of Population: State Formation, Statistics, and the Census of Canada, 1840-1875.* Toronto: University of Toronto Press, 2001.

–. "Social Investment in Medical Forms: The 1866 Cholera Scare and Beyond." *Canadian Historical Review* 81, 3 (2000): 347-79.

–. *True Government by Choice Men? Inspection, Education, and State Formation in Canada West.* Toronto: University of Toronto Press, 1992.

Davey, Ian E. "School Reform and School Attendance: The Hamilton Central School, 1853-1861." In *Education and Social Change: Themes from Ontario's Past,* edited by Michael B. Katz and Paul H. Mattingly, 294-314. New York: New York University Press, 1975.

Davidoff, Leonore, and Catherine Hall. *Family Fortunes: Men and Women of the English Middle Class, 1780-1850.* Chicago: University of Chicago Press, 1987.

Dekker, Jeroen J.H. "Transforming the Nation and the Child: Philanthropy in the Netherlands, Belgium, France and England, c. 1780-c. 1850." In *Charity, Philanthropy and Reform from the 1690s to 1850s,* edited by Hugh Cunningham and Joanna Innes, 130-47. London: Macmillan Press Limited, 1998.

Doucet, Michael, and John C. Weaver. "Town Fathers and Urban Continuity: The Roots of Community Power and Physical Form in Hamilton, Upper Canada, in the 1830s." In *Historical Essays on Upper Canada: New Perspectives,* edited by J.K. Johnson and Bruce G. Wilson, 425-59. Ottawa: Carleton University Press, 1989.

Downs, Susan Whitelaw, and Michael W. Sherraden. "The Orphan Asylum in the Nineteenth Century." *Social Service Review* 57, 2 (1983): 272-90.

Dulberger, Judith A. *"Mother Donit fore the Best": Correspondence of a Nineteenth-Century Orphan Asylum.* Syracuse, NY: Syracuse University Press, 1996.

Engels, Frederick. *Origins of the Family, Private Property and the State.* 1884. Edited by Eleanor Burke Leacock. New York: International Publishers, 1972.

Errington, Elizabeth Jane. *Wives and Mothers, Schoolmistresses and Scullery Maids: Working Women in Upper Canada 1790-1840.* Montreal and Kingston: McGill-Queen's University Press, 1995.

Fecteau, Jean-Marie. *La liberté du pauvre: Crime et pauvreté au XIXe siècle québécois.* Montreal: VLB Éditeur, 2004.

Fecteau, Jean-Marie, and Éric Vaillancourt. "The Saint Vincent de Paul Society and the Catholic Charitable System in Quebec (1846-1921)." In *The Churches and Social Order in Nineteenth- and Twentieth-Century Canada,* edited by Michael Gauvreau and Ollivier Hubert, 195-224. Montreal and Kingston: McGill-Queen's University Press, 2006.

Ferry, Darren. *Uniting in Measures of Common Good: The Construction of Liberal Identities in Central Canada.* Montreal and Kingston: McGill-Queen's University Press, 2008.

Fingard, Judith. *The Dark Side of Life in Victorian Halifax.* Halifax, NS: Pottersfield Press, 1989.

Fraser, Nancy. "Rethinking the Public Sphere: A Contribution to the Critique of Actually Existing Democracy." In *Habermas and the Public Sphere,* edited by Craig Calhoun, 110-34. Cambridge, MA: MIT Press, 1992.

–. "What's Critical about Critical Theory? The Case of Habermas and Gender." *New German Critique* 35 (Spring/Summer 1985): 97-131.

Gauvreau, Michael. *The Evangelical Century: College and Creed in English Canada from the Great Revival to the Great Depression.* Montreal and Kingston: McGill-Queen's University Press, 1991.

–. "Forging a New Space for Lay Male Piety: St. Vincent de Paul Societies in Urban Quebec and Ontario, 1846-1890." *Histoire Sociale/Social History* 42, 83 (2009): 35-67.

–. "Protestantism Transformed: Personal Piety and the Evangelical Social Vision, 1815-1867." In *The Canadian Protestant Experience 1760-1990,* edited by George A. Rawlyk, 48-97. Montreal and Kingston: McGill-Queen's University Press, 1990.

Ginzberg, Lori D. *Women and the Work of Benevolence: Morality, Politics, and Class in the Nineteenth-Century United States.* New Haven, CT: Yale University Press, 1990.

Gordon, Eleanor, and Gwyneth Nair. *Public Lives: Women, Family and Society in Victorian Britain.* New Haven, CT: Yale University Press, 2003.

Gordon, Linda. *Pitied but Not Entitled: Single Mothers and the History of Welfare: 1890-1935.* New York: Free Press, 1994.

Grant, John Webster. *A Profusion of Spires: Religion in Nineteenth-Century Ontario.* Toronto: University of Toronto Press, 1988.

Greenfield, Katherine. "The Reverend John Gamble Geddes and Early Days at Christ's Church Hamilton." *Wentworth Bygones* 4 (1963): 9-21.

Greer, Allan, and Ian Radforth, eds. *Colonial Leviathan: State Formation in Mid-Nineteenth-Century Canada.* Toronto: University of Toronto Press, 1992.

Grossberg, Michael. *Governing the Hearth: Law and Family in Nineteenth-Century America.* Chapel Hill: University of North Carolina Press, 1985.

Habermas, Jürgen. *The Structural Transformation of the Public Sphere: An Inquiry into the Category of Bourgeois Society.* Translated by Thomas Burger with assistance from Frederick Lawrence. Cambridge, MA: MIT Press, 1989.

Harvey, Janice. "The Protestant Orphan Asylum and the Montreal Ladies' Benevolent Society: A Case Study in Protestant Child Charity in Montreal, 1822-1900." PhD diss., McGill University, 2001.

Hasci, Timothy. *Second Home: Orphan Asylums and Poor Families in America.* Cambridge, MA: Harvard University Press, 1997.

Henley, Brian. *1846 Hamilton: From a Frontier Town to the Ambitious City.* Hamilton: North Shore Publishing, 1995.

Hewitt, Nancy. *Women's Activism and Social Change, Rochester, New York, 1822-1872.* Ithaca, NY: Cornell University Press, 1984.

Holman, Andrew C. *A Sense of Their Duty: Middle-Class Formation in Victorian Ontario Towns.* Montreal and Kingston: McGill-Queen's University Press, 2000.

Houston, Susan. "Impetus to Reform: Urban Crime, Poverty and Ignorance in Ontario, 1850-1875." PhD diss., University of Toronto, 1974.

Houston, Susan, and Alison Prentice. *Schooling and Scholars in Nineteenth-Century Ontario.* Toronto: University of Toronto Press, 1988.

Isenberg, Nancy. *Sex and Citizenship in Antebellum America.* Chapel Hill: University of North Carolina Press, 1998.

Jones, Andrew, and Leonard Rutman. *In the Children's Aid: J.J. Kelso and Child Welfare in Ontario.* Toronto: University of Toronto Press, 1981.

Katz, Michael. *In the Shadow of the Poorhouse: A Social History of Welfare in America.* New York: Basic Books, 1996.

–. *The People of Hamilton, Canada West: Family and Class in a Mid-Nineteenth-Century City.* Cambridge, MA: Harvard University Press, 1975.

Kaufman, James. "Corporate Law and the Sovereignty of States." *American Sociological Review* 73 (June 2008): 402-25.

Kealey, G.S. "Orangemen and the Corporation: The Politics of Class during the Union of the Canadas." In *Forging a Consensus: Historical Essays on Toronto,* edited by V.L. Russell, 41-86. Toronto: University of Toronto Press, 1984.

Kerber, Linda. "Separate Spheres, Female Worlds, Woman's Place: The Rhetoric of Women's History." *Journal of American History* 75, 1 (1988): 9-39.

Kidd, Alan. *State, Society, and the Poor in Nineteenth-Century England.* New York: St. Martin's Press, 1999.

Koven, Seth, and Sonya Michel, eds. *Mothers of a New World: Maternalist Politics and the Origins of Welfare States.* New York: Routledge, 1993.

Kristofferson, Robert. *Craft Capitalism: Craftworkers and Early Industrialization in Hamilton, 1840-1870.* Toronto: University of Toronto Press, 2007.

Landes, Joan B. *Women and the Public Sphere in the Age of French Revolution.* Ithaca, NY: Cornell University Press, 1988.

Lawes, Carolyn J. *Women and Reform in a New England Community, 1815-1860.* Lexington: University Press of Kentucky, 2000.

Lebsock, Suzanne. *The Free Women of Petersburg: Status and Culture in a Southern Town, 1784-1860.* New York: W.W. Norton, 1984.

Little, J.I. *State and Society in Transition: The Politics of Institutional Reform in the Eastern Townships, 1838-1852.* Montreal and Kingston: McGill-Queen's University Press, 1997.

Little, Margaret Jane Hillyard. *"No Car, No Radio, No Liquor Permit": The Moral Regulation of Single Mothers in Ontario, 1920-1997.* Toronto: Oxford University Press, 1998.

Luddy, Maria. *Women and Philanthropy in Nineteenth-Century Ireland.* Cambridge, UK: Cambridge University Press, 1995.

Mah, Harold. "Phantasies of the Public Sphere: Rethinking the Habermas of Historians." *Journal of Modern History* 72 (March 2000): 153-82.

Mandler, Peter. "Poverty and Charity in the Nineteenth-Century Metropolis: An Introduction." In *The Uses of Charity: The Poor on Relief in the Nineteenth-Century Metropolis,* edited by Peter Mandler, 1-37. Philadelphia: University of Pennsylvania Press, 1990.

Maurutto, Paula. *Governing Charities: Church and State in Toronto's Catholic Archdiocese 1850s to 1950s.* Montreal and Kingston: McGill-Queen's University Press, 2003.

McCalla, Douglas. *Planting the Province: The Economic History of Upper Canada 1784-1870.* Toronto: University of Toronto Press, 1993.

McCarthy, Kathleen D. *American Creed: Philanthropy and the Rise of Civil Society, 1700-1865.* Chicago: University of Chicago Press, 2003.

–. *Noblesse Oblige: Charity and Cultural Philanthropy in Chicago, 1849-1929.* Chicago: University of Chicago Press, 1982.

–, ed. *Lady Bountiful Revisited: Women, Philanthropy and Power.* New Brunswick, NJ: Rutgers University Press, 1990.

McKay, Ian. "Canada as Long Liberal Revolution: On Writing the History of Actually Existing Canadian Liberalisms, 1840s-1940s." In *Liberalism and Hegemony: Debating the Liberal Revolution,* edited by Jean-François Constant and Michel Ducharme, 347-452. Toronto: University of Toronto Press, 2009.

–. "The Liberal Order Framework: A Prospectus for a Reconnaissance of Canadian History." *Canadian Historical Review* 81, 4 (2000): 617-45.

McNairn, Jeffrey L. *The Capacity to Judge: Public Opinion and Deliberative Democracy in Upper Canada, 1791-1854.* Toronto: University of Toronto Press, 2000.

Meehan, Johanna, ed. *Feminists Read Habermas: Gendering the Subject of Discourse.* New York: Routledge, 1995.

Melder, Keith. "Ladies Bountiful: Organized Women's Benevolence in Early 19th-century America." *New York History* 48, 3 (July 1967): 231-54.

Mintz, Steven, and Susan Kellogg. *Domestic Revolutions: A Social History of American Family Life.* New York: Free Press, 1988.

Mitchinson, Wendy. "The WCTU: 'For God, Home and Native Land': A Study in Nineteenth-Century Feminism." In *A Not Unreasonable Claim: Women and Reform in Canada, 1880s-1920s,* edited by Linda Kealey, 151-67. Toronto: Women's Press, 1979.

Morgan, Cecilia. *Public Men and Virtuous Women: The Gendered Languages of Religion and Politics in Upper Canada, 1791-1850.* Toronto: University of Toronto Press, 1996.

Neff, Charlotte. "The Education of Destitute Homeless Children in Nineteenth-Century Ontario." *Journal of Family History* 29, 1 (2004): 3-46.

–. "Government Approaches to Child Neglect and Mistreatment in Nineteenth-Century Ontario." *Histoire Sociale/Social History* 41, 81 (2008): 165-214.

–. "Pauper Apprenticeship in Early Nineteenth Century Ontario." *Journal of Family History* 21, 2 (1996): 144-71.

–. "The Role of Protestant Children's Homes in Nineteenth-Century Ontario: Child Rescue or Family Support?" *Journal of Family History* 34, 1 (2009): 48-88.

Noel, Jan. "Women and Social Welfare in the Montreal Region, 1800-1833: Preliminary Findings." In *Changing Roles of Women with the Christian Church in Canada*, edited by Elizabeth G. Muir and Marilyn F. Whiteley, 261-83. Toronto: University of Toronto Press, 1995.

Norton, Mary Beth. *Founding Mothers and Fathers: Gendered Power and the Forming of American Society*. New York: A.A. Knopf, 1996.

Owen, David. *English Philanthropy, 1660-1960*. Cambridge, MA: Harvard University Press, 1964.

Palmer, Bryan D. *A Culture in Conflict: Skilled Workers and Industrial Capitalism in Hamilton, Ontario, 1860-1914*. Montreal and Kingston: McGill-Queen's University Press, 1979.

–. *Working-Class Experience: The Rise and Reconstitution of Canadian Labour, 1800-1980*. Toronto: Butterworth and Co., 1983.

Parr, G.J. "The Welcome and the Wake, Attitudes in Canada West toward the Irish Famine Migration." *Ontario History* 66, 2 (1974): 101-13.

Parr, Joy. *Labouring Children: British Immigrant Apprentices to Canada, 1869-1924*. Montreal and Kingston: McGill-Queen's University Press, 1980.

Pateman, Carole. "Feminist Critiques of the Public/Private Dichotomy." In *Feminism and Equality*, edited by Anne Phillips, 103-26. New York: New York University Press, 1987.

–. *The Sexual Contract: Aspects of Patriarchal Liberalism*. Stanford: Stanford University Press, 1988.

Pinchbeck, Ivy, and Margaret Hewitt. *Children in English Society*. Vol. 2, *From the Eighteenth Century to the Children Act 1948*. London: Routledge and Kegan Paul, 1973.

Porter, Susan. "The Benevolent Asylum – Image and Reality: The Care and Training of Female Orphans in Boston, 1800-1840." PhD diss., Boston University, 1984.

–. "A Good Home: Indenture and Adoption in Nineteenth-Century Orphanages." In *Adoption in America: Historical Perspectives*, edited by E. Wayne Carp, 27-50. Ann Arbor: University of Michigan Press, 2002.

Prochaska, F.K. *Women and Philanthropy in Nineteenth-Century England*. Oxford: Clarendon Press, 1980.

Riley, Denise. *"Am I that Name?" Feminism and the Category of "Women" in History*. London: Macmillan Press, 1988.

Roberts, Michael J.D. "Head versus Heart? Voluntary Associations and Charity Organization in England, c. 1700-1850." In *Charity, Philanthropy and Reform from the 1690s to 1850*, edited by Hugh Cunningham and Joanna Innes, 66-86. London: Macmillan Press, 1998.

Rooke, Patricia T., and R.L. Schnell. "Childhood and Charity in Nineteenth-Century British North America." *Histoire Sociale/Social History* 15, 29 (1982): 157-79.

–. *Discarding the Asylum: From Child Rescue to the Welfare State in English Canada (1800-1950)*. Lanham, MD: University Press of America, 1983.

–. "Guttersnipes and Charity Children: Nineteenth Century Child Rescue in the Atlantic Provinces." In *Studies in Childhood History: A Canadian Perspective*, edited by Patricia T. Rooke and R.L. Schnell, 82-104. Calgary: Detselig Enterprises, 1982.

–. "The Rise and Decline of British North American Protestant Orphan's Homes as Woman's Domain, 1850-1930." *Atlantis* 7, 2 (1982): 21-35.

Rosaldo, Michelle Zimbalist. "The Use and Abuse of Anthropology: Reflections on Feminism and Cross-Cultural Understanding." *Signs* 5, 3 (1980): 389-417.

–. "Woman, Culture and Society: A Theoretical Overview." In *Woman, Culture and Society,* edited by Michelle Zimbalist Rosaldo and Louise Lamphere, 17-42. Stanford: Stanford University Press, 1974.

Rose, Nikolas, and Peter Miller. "Political Power beyond the State: Problematics of Government." *British Journal of Sociology* 43, 2 (1992): 173-205.

Rothenberg, Winifred. *From Market Places to a Market Economy: The Transformation of Rural Massachusetts, 1750-1850.* Chicago: University of Chicago Press, 1992.

Rothman, David J. *The Discovery of the Asylum: Social Order and Disorder in the New Republic.* Boston: Little, Brown and Co., 1971.

Ryan, Mary P. *The Cradle of the Middle Class: The Family in Oneida County, New York, 1790-1865.* Cambridge: Cambridge University Press, 1981.

–. "Gender and Public Access: Women's Politics in Nineteenth-Century America." In *Habermas and the Public Sphere,* edited by Craig Calhoun, 259-88. Cambridge, MA: MIT Press, 1992.

–. *Women in Public: Between Banners and Ballots, 1825-1880.* Baltimore: Johns Hopkins University Press, 1990.

Scott, Anne Firor. *Natural Allies: Women's Associations in American History.* Urbana: University of Illinois Press, 1991.

Scott, Joan Wallach. *Gender and the Politics of History.* New York: Columbia University Press, 1988.

See, Scott. "The Orange Order and Social Violence in Mid-Nineteenth-Century Saint John." *Acadiensis* 13 (Autumn 1983): 68-92.

Semple, Neil. "'The Nurture and Admonition of the Lord': Nineteenth-Century Canadian Methodism's Response to Childhood." *Histoire Sociale/Social History* 14, 27 (1981): 157-75.

Sherman, Sandra. *Imagining Poverty: Quantification and the Decline of Paternalism.* Columbus: Ohio State University Press, 2001.

Siena, Kevin. "Hospitals for the Excluded or Convalescent Homes? Workhouses, Medicalization and the Poor Law in Long Eighteenth-Century London and Pre-Confederation Toronto." *Canadian Bulletin of Medical History* 27, 1 (2010): 5-25.

Sklar, Kathryn Kish. *Catharine Beecher: A Study in American Domesticity.* New York: W.W. Norton and Company, 1976.

Skocpol, Theda. *Protecting Soldiers and Mothers: The Political Origins of Social Policy in the United States.* Cambridge, MA: Belknap Press of Harvard University Press, 1992.

Smandych, Russell C. "William Osgoode, John Graves Simcoe and the Exclusion of the English Poor Law from Upper Canada." In *Law, Society and the State: Essays in Modern Legal History,* edited by Louis Knafla and Susan W.S. Binnie, 99-128. Toronto: University of Toronto Press, 1995.

Smith-Rosenberg, Carroll. *Religion and the Rise of the American City: The New York City Mission Movement, 1812-1870.* Ithaca, NY: Cornell University Press, 1971.

Splane, Richard B. *Social Welfare in Ontario, 1791-1893: A Study of Public Welfare Administration.* Toronto: University of Toronto Press, 1965.

Strong-Boag, Veronica. *Finding Families, Finding Ourselves: English Canada Encounters Adoption from the Nineteenth Century to the 1990s.* Don Mills, ON: Oxford University Press, 2006.

–. *Fostering Nation? Canada Confronts Its History of Childhood Disadvantage.* Waterloo, ON: Wilfrid Laurier University Press, 2011.

Summers, Anne. "A Home from Home – Women's Philanthropic Work in the Nineteenth Century." In *Fit Work for Women,* edited by Sandra Burman, 33-63. New York: St. Martin's Press, 1979.

Sutherland, David A. "Voluntary Societies and the Process of Middle-Class Formation in Early Victorian Halifax, Nova Scotia." *Journal of the Canadian Historical Association* 5, 1 (1994): 237-63.

Sutherland, Neil. *Children in English-Canadian Society: Framing the Twentieth-Century Consensus.* Toronto: University of Toronto Press, 1976.

Trigger, Rosalyn. "Irish Politics on Parade: The Clergy, National Societies, and St. Patrick's Day Processions in Nineteenth-Century Montreal and Toronto." *Histoire Sociale/Social History* 37, 74 (2004): 159-99.

Valverde, Mariana. *The Age of Light, Soap and Water: Moral Reform in English Canada, 1885-1925.* Toronto: McClelland and Stewart, 1991.

–. "The Mixed Social Economy as Canadian Tradition." *Studies in Political Economy* 47 (Summer 1995): 33-59.

Van der Klein, Marian, Rebecca Jo Plant, Nichole Sanders, and Lori R. Weintrob, eds. *Maternalism Reconsidered: Motherhood, Welfare and Social Policy in the Twentieth Century.* New York: Berghahn Books, 2012.

Van Die, Marguerite. *An Evangelical Mind: Nathanael Burwash and the Methodist Tradition in Canada, 1839-1918.* Montreal and Kingston: McGill-Queen's University Press, 1989.

–. "Revisiting 'Separate Spheres': Women, Religion, and the Family in Mid-Victorian Brantford, Ontario." In *Households of Faith: Family, Gender and Community in Canada, 1760-1969,* edited by Nancy Christie, 234-63. Montreal and Kingston: McGill-Queen's University Press, 2001.

Varty, Carmen Nielson. "'A Career in Christian Charity': Women's Benevolence and the Public Sphere in a Mid-Nineteenth-Century Canadian City." *Women's History Review* 14, 2 (2005): 243-64.

Ward, W. Peter. "Unwed Motherhood in Nineteenth-Century English Canada." *Historical Papers* (1981): 34-56.

Weaver, John C. *Crimes, Constables, and Courts: Order and Transgression in a Canadian City, 1816-1970.* Montreal and Kingston: McGill-Queen's University Press, 1995.

–. *Hamilton: An Illustrated History.* Toronto: James Lorimer and Company, 1982.

Welter, Barbara. "The Cult of True Womanhood, 1820-1860." *American Quarterly* 18 (Summer 1966): 151-74.

White, Robert, and Dallas Hanson. "Rationality and Rhetoric in the Corporate World: The Corporate Annual Report as an Aristotelian Genre." *Prometheus* 18, 3 (2000): 303-17.

Yeo, Eileen Janes. *The Contest for Social Science: Relations and Representations of Gender and Class.* London: Rivers Oram Press, 1996.

–, ed. *Radical Femininity: Women's Self-representation in the Public Sphere.* Manchester: Manchester University Press, 1998.

Zaeske, Susan. *Signatures of Citizenship: Petitioning, Antislavery, and Women's Political Identity.* Chapel Hill: University of North Carolina Press, 2003.

Zelizer, Viviana A. Rotman. *Pricing the Priceless Child: The Changing Social Value of Children.* New York: Basic Books, 1985.

Index

Note: "(f)" after a page number indicates a figure; "HOA/LBS" stands for Hamilton Orphan Asylum and Ladies' Benevolent Society; "LBS," for Ladies' Benevolent Society; "RC," for Roman Catholic

Printed in Canada

Set in Galliard and New Baskerville by Artegraphica Design Co. Ltd.

Copy editor: Joanne Muzak

Proofreader: Lana Okerlund

Indexer: Patricia Buchanan